Celebrate Fish

Members' Greatest Recipes

NORTH AMERICAN FISHING CLUB ®

Minnetonka   Minnesota

Celebrate Fish
Members' Greatest Recipes

Printed in 2008.

Tom Carpenter
Creative Director

Jen Weaverling
Managing Editor

Teresa Marrone
Book Production

Bill Lindner Photography
Commissoned Photography

Robin Krause
Susan Telleen
Recipe Selection

Abigail Wyckoff
Food Stylist

Mike Hehner and Steve Schenten
Photo Assistants

Special thanks to: *Mike Billstein, Terry Casey, Janice Cauley, Nancy Maurer and Ruth Petran.*

On cover: *Mom's Best Crappie Sandwich, page 98.*

3 4 5 6 7 8 9 10 / 10 09 08
© 2006 North American Fishing Club
ISBN 10: 1-58159-277-9
ISBN 13: 978-1-58159-277-1

North American Fishing Club

12301 Whitewater Drive
Minnetonka, MN 55343
www.fishingclub.com

Special Note: The North American Fishing Club proudly presents this special cookbook edition which includes the personal favorites of your fellow members. Each recipe has been screened by a cooking professional and edited for clarity. However, we are not able to kitchen-test these recipes and cannot guarantee their outcome, or your safety in their preparation or consumption. Please be advised that any recipes which require the use of dangerous equipment (such as pressure cookers) or potentially unsafe preparation procedures (such as canning and pickling) should be used with caution and safe, healthy practices.

Contents

Cook them up right and really *Celebrate Fish!*

While the catch-and-release ethic is alive and well among North American Fishing Club Members, it's also true that there's not a problem in saving a few delicious fish to eat now and then, when regulations permit. When you do keep a few, it's cause for celebration! You get to celebrate a fine day of fishing one more time when you eat a wonderful meal that features your catch. And when you use a great recipe and prepare the fish with care and respect, you celebrate the fish itself. That's what *Celebrate Fish* is all about! Here are dozens upon dozens of *Members' Greatest Recipes,* presented to you in one beautiful package. You'll also get insiders' instruction on general fish cooking techniques (for when you want to cook up your catch on your own), and a full set of delightful menus (complete with all the side dish recipes) to help you create complete fish meals to remember. So get fishing, get cooking ... and *Celebrate Fish!*

Deep Fried

FRIED SUNFISH

Jim Molsbee
Lumberton, Mississippi

2 medium onions, sliced
6 (about 6 oz. each) sunfish fillets
2 cups salt
3 tablespoons cayenne pepper
1 cup cornmeal

❶ Cover bottom of baking dish or large bowl with onions. Place layer of sunfish over onions; sprinkle with a light coating of salt and cayenne pepper. Repeat layers. Sprinkle top layer of sunfish with remaining generous amount of cayenne pepper and salt.

❷ Place baking dish in refrigerator, let sit 8 hours. Rinse sunfish; discard onions and spices. Dredge fillets in cornmeal; fry at 375°F 3 to 5 minutes or until golden brown and flaky on the inside.

6 servings.

BATTERED WALLEYE

Frank V. Jovenall
Sharpsville, Pennsylvania

3 lbs. skinned walleye fillets, cut into 5-inch pieces
1 quart buttermilk
1 slice lemon
1½ pints vegetable oil
3 cups pancake mix
2½ cups club soda

❶ Soak fillets in enough buttermilk and lemon slice to cover completely; refrigerate 2 hours.

❷ Heat oil in large, heavy saucepan and heat oven to 250°F.

❸ Remove fillets from marinade; discard marinade. In large bowl, dredge fillets in 1 cup of the pancake mix. In another large bowl, combine remaining 2 cups of the pancake mix with club soda; mix to consistency of buttermilk. Dip fillets in batter; let excess drip back into bowl. Deep fry 4 minutes per side or until golden brown and fish flakes easily with a fork.

❹ Keep fish warm on baking sheet in oven until all are cooked. Serve with seasoned fries.

6 servings.

POTATO FLAKED WALLEYE

Abby Wilson
Chanhassen, Minnesota

⅔ cup all-purpose flour

¼ teaspoon salt

1 teaspoon paprika

¼ teaspoon freshly ground pepper

¼ teaspoon onion powder

1 garlic clove, minced

1 cup potato flakes

2 eggs

6 (about 6 oz. each) walleye fillets

Olive oil

❶ In medium dish, combine flour, salt, paprika, pepper, onion powder and garlic. Add potato flakes to a second dish. In large bowl, beat 2 eggs. Dredge fillets in this order: flour, beaten eggs and potato flakes.

❷ In large, heavy skillet, heat ¼ inch oil over medium heat until hot. Add fillets; fry 5 to 7 minutes, turning once, or until golden brown and fish flakes easily with a fork. Drain on paper-towel-lined plate. Serve with lemon wedge and tartar sauce.

6 servings.

BEER BATTER FILLETS

Shari Vermeer
Big Lake, Missouri

1 cup beer

1 egg

½ cup all-purpose flour

1 teaspoon parsley flakes

1½ lbs. walleye, crappie, perch or bluegill fillets, dried and dusted with flour

1¼ cups potato flakes

Peanut or vegetable oil for frying

Seasoned salt to taste

❶ In large bowl, mix beer, egg, flour and parsley flakes. Dip fillets in batter, then potato flakes.

❷ In large, heavy skillet, heat ¼ inch oil over medium-high heat until hot. Add fillets; fry 3 to 5 minutes, turning once, or until golden brown and fish flakes easily with a fork. Drain on paper towel. Season with salt.

4 servings.

CRUNCH FRIED WALLEYE

Edward Goans
Parma, Ohio

1 egg

1 cup evaporated milk

2 cups cracker crumbs

⅛ teaspoon salt

⅛ teaspoon freshly ground pepper

1½ lbs. walleye fillets

2 to 4 tablespoons vegetable oil

❶ In large bowl, blend egg and milk. In another large bowl, combine crackers, salt and pepper. Dip fillets in egg mixture, then cracker crumbs.

❷ In large skillet, heat oil over medium-high heat until hot. Add fillets; fry a few pieces at a time about 3 minutes per side, then turn. Fry an additional 2 to 3 minutes or until fish flakes easily with a fork.

4 servings.

DEEP FRIED
BLUEGILL BELLIES

**Roger D. McKeon
Penfield, New York**

1½ lbs. bluegill bellies
½ cup cornmeal
¼ cup all-purpose flour
½ teaspoon salt
½ teaspoon freshly ground black pepper
½ teaspoon cayenne pepper
½ teaspoon paprika
¼ teaspoon garlic powder

❶ Fillet bluegills with extra care to remove the thin covering of flesh over the rib cage. Separate this delicate portion of the fillet at the median line, and prepare for deep frying as follows: Rinse in cold water and dry sparingly with paper towels. Place in a paper bag with cornmeal, flour, salt, black pepper, red pepper, paprika and garlic powder.

❷ In large skillet, deep fry fillets in canola or peanut oil until golden brown and fish flakes easily with a fork. Drain on paper towel; let sit 15 to 30 minutes, then deep fry a second time. Enjoy them as is or dip in cocktail sauce, your choice.

6 servings.

BEER BATTERED
CRAPPIE

**Brandon Hogg
Aubrey, Texas**

1 cup all-purpose flour
1 cup cooking oil
1 teaspoon salt
1 teaspoon paprika
1 cup beer
1 egg
8 crappie fillets, patted dry and lightly salted

❶ In large bowl, mix flour, cooking oil, salt, paprika, beer and egg until smooth. Dip fillets in batter.

❷ In large, heavy skillet, heat ¼ inch oil over medium heat until hot. Add fillets; fry 5 to 7 minutes, turning once, or until golden brown and fish flakes easily with a fork. Drain on paper-towel-lined plate.

4 servings.

BEER BATTERED CRAPPIE

LAKE TEXOMA SPICY FISH

Carolyn Kinsey
Kingston, Oklahoma

1/2 cup yellow mustard

1 tablespoon cayenne pepper

1 tablespoon garlic salt

1 tablespoon Tabasco sauce

1/2 teaspoon freshly ground black pepper

2 lbs. catfish, crappie, sandbass, largemouth bass, and smallmouth bass, cut into 1 1/2-inch pieces

1 cup all-purpose flour

1 cup yellow cornmeal

Oil for frying

Jalapeño peppers

❶ In large bowl, combine yellow mustard, cayenne pepper, garlic salt, Tabasco and black pepper. Coat fish pieces in mixture, then refrigerate 2 to 4 hours. Remove fish pieces from mixture; discard mixture. Coat fish pieces with flour and cornmeal.

❷ In large frying pan, heat oil over medium heat until hot. Add fish; cook 3 to 4 minutes on each side or until golden brown and fish flakes easily with a fork. Serve with additional hot sauce or jalapeño peppers.

4 servings.

SIMPLE CATFISH

Kenneth Anthony
Grantville, Kansas

4 (about 8 oz. each) catfish fillets, cut into 1 1/2-inch pieces

1 (12-oz.) can 7-Up or lemon-flavored beverage

1 cup white corn meal

1 teaspoon salt

1/2 teaspoon freshly ground pepper

Oil for deep frying

❶ Dip fillet in 7-Up. In large, resealable plastic bag, combine cornmeal, salt and pepper. Add fillets; shake to coat. Remove fillets; discard cornmeal mixture.

❷ Fry in 375°F oil 3 to 5 minutes or until golden brown and fish flakes easily with a fork.

4 servings.

PANCAKE BATTERED FISH

Steve Hartlaben
Pulaski, Wisconsin

1 egg

1/4 cup milk

1 cup pancake mix

1 tablespoon seasoning salt

1 lb. walleye fillets

2 tablespoons vegetable oil

❶ In large bowl, mix egg and milk together. In brown paper bag, mix pancake mix and seasoning salt together. Dip fillets into egg mixture, then add to brown paper bag; shake to coat.

❷ In large skillet, heat oil over medium-high heat until hot. Add fillets; cook until fish flakes easily with a fork.

2 servings.

BEER BATTER

Jim Bullock
Mancelona, Michigan

1 cup Bisquick

1 egg

Salt to taste

1 cup beer

2 lbs. fish fillets

❶ In large bowl, mix Bisquick, egg and salt. Gradually add beer to desired consistency. Dredge fish in batter; deep fry.

4 servings.

CAJUN FRIED WALLEYE OR BASS

Frank E. Doyle
Hudson, Ohio

½ cup Bisquick

¼ cup milk

1 egg

1 cup cornmeal

2 teaspoons Cajun seasoning

¼ teaspoon salt

1½ lbs. walleye or bass fillets

Oil for frying

❶ In medium bowl, whisk together Bisquick, milk and egg.

❷ In shallow dish, mix cornmeal, Cajun seasoning and salt. Dip fillets into batter first, then dredge in cornmeal mixture. Fry fillets in hot oil, turning once, until golden brown and fish flakes easily with a fork. Drain on paper towels and serve. Ranch dressing makes a great dipping sauce for this.

4 servings.

BURGER BATTER-FRIED FISH

Richard Engstrom
Atwater, Minnesota

10 lbs. walleye fillets

1 dozen eggs

1 teaspoon freshly ground pepper

1 teaspoon garlic powder

1 teaspoon salt

1 tablespoon soy sauce

¾ box Ritz crackers

¼ box saltines

4 cups vegetable oil

¼ cup lemon juice

❶ Cube fillets to hamburger-bun size. Mix eggs, pepper, garlic powder, salt and soy sauce in large bowl. Add cubed fish, stir and set aside.

❷ In blender, blend Ritz crackers and saltines to fine mixture. In large frying pan, heat half of the oil over medium heat until hot. Roll fillet cubes in dry mixture, then fry until golden brown and fish flakes easily with a fork. Remove from pan. Keep adding oil so fish is half submerged. Add remaining fish to pan and continue until fish flakes easily with a fork.

❸ Place fried fish on plates with paper towels to absorb excess oil. When done, sprinkle with lemon juice.

24 servings.

CATFISH NIBLETS

Abby Wilson
Chanhassen, Minnesota

1/2 cup all-purpose flour

1/2 cup cornmeal

Choice of 1/4 teaspoon each salt, freshly ground pepper,
    cayenne pepper, onion or garlic powder

1 large yellow onion, cut into 1/4-inch strips

1 large red bell pepper, cut into 1/4-inch strips

1 large yellow bell pepper, cut into 1/4-inch strips

6 (about 6 oz. each) catfish fillets, cut into
    1 1/2-inch pieces

Olive oil

❶ In small bowl, combine flour, cornmeal, salt, pepper, cayenne, onion or garlic powder. Dust onion, peppers and fish with seasoning mix.

❷ In large skillet, heat 1/2 inch oil over medium heat until hot. Add fish a few at a time; fry 3 to 5 minutes or until golden brown and fish flakes easily with a fork. Drain on paper towels.

6 servings

BEER BATTER SALMON

Jerome Bowerman
Canajoharie, New York

1 cup all-purpose flour

1 tablespoon salt

1 tablespoon paprika

1 (12-oz.) can beer

2 lbs. salmon fillets

Vegetable oil

❶ In large bowl, mix flour, salt, paprika and a portion of the beer together. If batter becomes too thick, thin with beer. Cut salmon into cubes.

❷ In frying pan, heat oil to 375°F.

❸ Dip salmon cubes into beer batter and allow to drain. Deep fry cubes 5 or 6 at a time until golden brown and fish flakes easily with a fork.

4 servings.

FRIED WHITING FISH FILLETS

Allen Fitzpatrick
Wyoming, Michigan

1 cup canola cooking oil

2 cups yellow cornmeal

1/2 teaspoon lemon pepper

1/2 teaspoon freshly ground black pepper

1/4 teaspoon cayenne pepper

1 teaspoon parsley flakes

1/4 teaspoon garlic salt

5 lbs. whiting fish fillets

❶ In large frying pan, heat oil over medium heat until hot.

❷ In large bowl, combine cornmeal, lemon pepper, black pepper, cayenne pepper, parsley flakes and salt. Coat both sides of fillets with cornmeal mixture; cook approximately 3 minutes on each side or until golden brown and fish flakes easily with a fork. Drain on paper towels.

10 servings

DEEP FRIED BUTTERMILK BATTERED FISH

Gerald Kuehn
Wautoma, Wisconsin

1 cup buttermilk
1 egg, beaten
6 walleye fillets, 10 perch fillets, or 30 smelt
1 1/2 cups crushed crackers
Vegetable oil

❶ In large bowl, combine buttermilk with beaten egg. Wash and dry fish fillets. Dip fillets in batter, then in crackers. Place fillets on parchment paper-lined baking sheet. (Fish may be placed in refrigerator until cooking time.) Deep fry in hot oil 6 to 7 minutes or until golden brown and fish flakes easily with a fork. For pan frying, pour oil into pan until 1/4 to 1/2 inch deep. Fry fish 3 to 4 minutes on each side or until golden brown and fish flakes easily with a fork.

6 servings.

DEEP FRIED COCONUT ALASKAN HALIBUT

Dick Deno
Black River Falls, Wisconsin

1 cup buttermilk pancake mix
1 can beer, if desired to create beer batter
1/2 cup flaked coconut, finely chopped
2 lbs. halibut, cut into 1 1/2-inch pieces
Canola oil

❶ Prepare buttermilk pancake mix according to package directions (if desired, use beer to create beer batter); stir in flaked coconut. Dip fish into buttermilk and pancake batter mix. In large frying pan, heat oil over medium heat until hot. Add fish; cook 3 to 4 minutes on each side or until golden brown and fish flakes easily with a fork. Serve with your favorite side dish and tartar sauce, if desired.

4 to 6 servings.

DEEP FRIED COCONUT ALASKAN HALIBUT

Baked
& Stuffed

SUN-DRIED TOMATO CRUSTED HALIBUT

SUN-DRIED TOMATO CRUSTED HALIBUT

David Wei
Vancouver, British Columbia, Canada

1 (4-oz.) pkg. sun-dried tomatoes

1 tablespoon chives, chopped

1 tablespoon capers, chopped

½ teaspoon freshly ground pepper

2 tablespoons olive oil

White wine

1½ lbs. halibut fillets, cut 1 inch thick

½ cup fine bread crumbs

1 tablespoon melted butter

¼ cup sliced toasted almonds

❶ Heat oven to 375°F. Spray 9x12-inch baking dish with nonstick cooking spray.

❷ Soak sun-dried tomatoes according to package directions, then coarsely chop. In large bowl, mix together chopped tomatoes, chives, capers, pepper and olive oil.

❸ Pour ¼ inch of white wine into bottom of dish. Place fillets in prepared baking dish. Spread tomato mixture evenly over fillets.

❹ In small bowl, combine bread crumbs and melted butter. Pour evenly over fillets. Sprinkle with sliced almonds. Bake 25 to 30 minutes or until fish is just opaque.

4 servings.

POLYNESIAN SALMON

William Capelle
Green Bay, Wisconsin

1 (6-oz.) can crushed pineapple

2 lbs. salmon fillets

Salt to taste

Freshly ground pepper to taste

½ medium onion, sliced

2 cups pea pods

¼ cup pickled ginger

Hot garlic ginger, if desired

❶ Heat oven to 400°F. Spray 13x9-inch baking dish with nonstick cooking spray.

❷ Spread pineapple evenly over bottom of prepared baking dish; top with salmon. Sprinkle with salt, pepper, onion, pea pods, ginger and hot garlic ginger. Bake 30 to 40 minutes or until fish flakes easily with a fork. Let stand 5 to 10 minutes before serving. Garnish with pineapple slices, if desired.

4 servings.

SOUR CREAM AND CHEESE BAKED HALIBUT

G. Michael Clemens
Fox Island, Washington

2 lbs. halibut fillets or steaks, 1½ inches thick

½ cup chopped green onions, including tops

1 cup sour cream

¼ teaspoon ground white pepper

½ teaspoon salt

⅓ cup Parmesan cheese

Dash of dill weed (optional)

❶ Heat oven to 350°F. Spray large, glass baking dish with nonstick cooking spray.

❷ Place halibut in prepared baking dish. In large bowl, combine onions, sour cream, pepper and salt. Pour mixture evenly over halibut. Bake 15 minutes, then sprinkle with cheese. Bake an additional 5 to 10 minutes or until fish flakes easily with a fork.

4 servings.

CHEESE TOPPED BAKED STEELHEAD

Frank V. Jovenall
Sharpsville, Pennsylvania

1½ lbs. steelhead fillets, cleaned

½ cup Miracle Whip

½ cup sour cream

2 tablespoons all-purpose flour

1½ teaspoons lemon juice

1 tablespoon minced onion

⅛ teaspoon cayenne pepper

½ cup (4 oz.) shredded cheddar cheese

❶ Heat oven to 425°F. Spray 8x12-inch baking dish with nonstick cooking spray.

❷ In medium bowl mix Miracle Whip, sour cream and flour until smooth. Stir in lemon juice, onion and cayenne pepper. Spoon mixture evenly over fish. Bake uncovered 12 to 14 minutes or until fish flakes easily with a fork. Sprinkle with cheese. Return baking dish to oven; cook an additional 2 minutes or until cheese is melted.

4 servings.

COCONUT CRUST TROUT OR SALMON

Dan Mitchell
Owasso, Oklahoma

4 (about 4 oz. each) trout or salmon fillets, skin removed

1 tablespoon lemon or lime juice

½ cup bread crumbs

½ cup shredded coconut

Salt to taste

Freshly ground pepper to taste

❶ Heat oven to 425°F. Place fillets on nonstick baking pan; brush on lemon or lime juice.

❷ In shallow bowl, combine bread crumbs, coconut, salt and pepper. Dredge fillets in bread crumb mixture and return them to prepared pan. Spread leftover mixture evenly over tops of fillets. Bake 12 to 15 minutes or until fish flakes easily with a fork.

4 servings.

BAKED STRIPED BASS

Donald Mansfield
Spring Creek, Nevada

4 slices of bacon, chopped

4 small white onions, thinly sliced

4 small celery hearts, cut in thin strips

1 small green bell pepper, chopped

2 tablespoons butter

1 tablespoon parsley

1 teaspoon freshly ground pepper

1 (2-lb.) striped bass

2 cups dry white wine

❶ Heat oven to 375°F. Spray large baking dish with nonstick cooking spray.

❷ In medium saucepan, sauté bacon until softened. Add onions, celery and green bell pepper; cook about 10 minutes. Add butter, parsley and pepper; blend well and cook an additional 5 minutes. Stuff fish with onion mixture.

❸ Place fish in prepared baking dish. Pour wine over fish; dot with butter. Bake 40 minutes or until fish flakes easily with a fork. Baste well every 10 minutes.

4 servings.

QUICK AND EASY BAKED SALMON

Earl Okuda
Salt Lake City, Utah

2 tablespoons butter
1 (1-lb.) salmon fillet
1 lemon
1 tablespoon lemon pepper
1 garlic clove, minced
2 fresh dill sprigs

❶ Heat oven to 350°F.

❷ Rub butter over large, heavy sheet of aluminum foil. Place salmon fillet skin-side down onto prepared foil. Squeeze one half of the lemon over salmon, reserving remaining half for garnish. Sprinkle with lemon pepper and garlic. Top with one sprig of fresh dill. Seal foil so that no moisture can escape. Bake 15 to 20 minutes or until fish flakes easily with a fork. Squeeze remaining one half of lemon over fish. Garnish with remaining fresh dill.

2 servings.

STUFFED WALLEYE

John R. Much
Perkasie, Pennsylvania

¼ cup chopped onion
½ cup chopped celery
1 cup each chopped green and red bell pepper
2 garlic cloves, minced
1 tablespoons butter
1 teaspoon Old Bay seasoning
½ cup mayonnaise
½ teaspoon dry mustard
2 dashes Worcestershire sauce
1 tablespoon chopped parsley
½ teaspoon freshly ground pepper
12 oz. crabmeat
1 large walleye fillet, filleted thin for each person

❶ Heat oven to 375°F.

❷ In large skillet, cook onion, celery, peppers and garlic in butter over medium heat until tender but not brown. Add Old Bay seasoning, mayonnaise, dry mustard, Worcestershire sauce, parsley, pepper and crabmeat; mix well.

❸ Place walleye fillets on aluminum foil and add several scoops of stuffing. Wrap fillets around stuffing and top with additional butter. Wrap tightly in aluminum foil and bake in oven 20 minutes or until fish flakes easily with a fork.

8 servings.

PARMESAN CATFISH

Karen Specht and John Hosking
Fountain City, Wisconsin

¾ cup milk

¼ cup beer

1 egg

¼ teaspoon baking soda

1 cup all-purpose flour

1 teaspoon Cajun spice

1 teaspoon salt

½ teaspoon freshly ground pepper

¼ teaspoon garlic powder

6 (8 to 10 oz. each) catfish, walleye, panfish or cod fillets

¼ cup grated Parmesan cheese

❶ Heat oven to 400°F.

❷ In medium bowl, beat together milk, beer, egg and baking soda. Let stand at least 5 minutes.

❸ In large, resealable plastic bag, mix flour, Cajun spice, salt, pepper and garlic powder. Dip fish in batter, then coat with flour mixture. Shake excess off for a light coating; discard remaining flour mixture.

❹ Place fillets on baking sheet; sprinkle with Parmesan cheese. Bake until fish flakes easily with a fork and cheese is browning at the edges.

6 servings.

ISLAND SPICED SALMON

Don Paradise
South Milwaukee, Wisconsin

2 tablespoons packed brown sugar

2 tablespoons chili powder

2 teaspoons ground cumin

1 teaspoon salt

½ teaspoon ground cinnamon

1 (2-lb.) salmon fillet

❶ Heat oven to 375°F. Spray 13x9-inch baking dish with nonstick cooking spray.

❷ In small bowl, combine brown sugar, chili powder, cumin, salt and cinnamon; mix well. Rub mixture evenly over flesh side of fillet; refrigerate 30 minutes.

❸ Arrange fillet skin-side down in prepared baking dish. Bake 20 to 25 minutes or until fish flakes easily with a fork.

8 servings.

ISLAND SPICED SALMON

EASY BAKED FISH PARMESAN

Dick Craig
Eden Prairie, Minnesota

2 lbs. fish fillets

1 cup sour cream

1/4 cup grated Parmesan cheese

1 tablespoon lemon juice

1 tablespoon grated onion

Dash of Tabasco sauce

Paprika

❶ Heat oven to 350°F. Spray 13x9-inch baking dish with nonstick cooking spray.

❷ Arrange fillets in prepared dish. In small bowl, mix together sour cream, Parmesan cheese, lemon juice, onion and Tabasco. Spread mixture evenly over fillets. Sprinkle with paprika. Bake 25 to 30 minutes or until fish flakes easily with a fork.

6 to 8 servings.

STUFFED BAKED TROUT

Brian Perkins
Pacific, Washington

1/2 onion, chopped and diced

2 garlic cloves, finely diced

1 1/2 tablespoons cubed butter

2 lbs. trout, cleaned and rinsed

Salt to taste

Freshly ground pepper to taste

❶ Heat oven to 350°F.

❷ In small bowl, mix together onion, garlic and cubed butter. Place fish on aluminum foil; stuff with onion mixture. Sprinkle with salt and pepper. Wrap fish in foil and bake about 30 to 40 minutes or until fish flakes easily with a fork.

4 servings.

BAKED HADDOCK

David Ostman
Deerfield, New Hampshire

1 1/2 lbs. boneless skinless haddock, cut into 4 pieces

1 cup buttermilk

1 cup Italian seasoned bread crumbs

1/2 cup grated Parmesan cheese

1/4 teaspoon thyme

Pinch of basil

1/4 cup melted butter

❶ Heat oven to 500°F. Spray large shallow baking dish with nonstick cooking spray.

❷ Place fish and buttermilk in large, resealable plastic bag. Refrigerate 1 to 2 hours. Remove fish from bag; discard buttermilk.

❸ In large bowl, mix together bread crumbs, Parmesan cheese, thyme and basil. Coat fish with bread crumb mixture. Place fish in a single layer in prepared baking dish. Slowly pour melted butter over fish. Bake about 10 to 15 minutes or until fish flakes easily with a fork.

4 servings.

CAJUN CATFISH

Matt O'Hara
St. Paul, Minnesota

3 strips bacon, chopped

2 garlic cloves, crushed

2 tablespoons chopped onion

4 tablespoons butter

1½ teaspoons Dijon mustard

2 teaspoons cayenne pepper

2 teaspoons Cajun seasoning

¼ teaspoon basil leaves

¼ teaspoon thyme

½ teaspoon oregano

5 drops Tabasco sauce

4 (6 to 8 oz. each) catfish, crappie or walleye fillets

❶ Heat oven to 375°F.

❷ In cast-iron skillet, sauté bacon, garlic and onion over medium heat until onions are translucent. Add butter, mustard, cayenne, Cajun spice, basil, thyme, oregano and Tabasco; simmer 3 minutes. Add fish; sauté 3 minutes or until brown. Place skillet in oven and bake 20 minutes or until fish flakes easily with a fork. Serve over white rice with Johnnycakes.

4 servings.

CREAM CHEESE WALLEYE

Shari Vermeer
Craig, Missouri

4 (6 to 8 oz. each) walleye fillets, cleaned

4 tablespoons lemon juice

1 (3-oz.) pkg. cream cheese

3 tablespoons chives, chopped

Seasoned salt to taste

❶ Heat oven to 350°F.

❷ Arrange fillets tightly side by side in 13x9-inch glass baking dish. Sprinkle with lemon juice. Cover with pats of cream cheese, chopped chives and seasoned salt to taste. Cover dish tightly with aluminum foil. Bake until fish is opaque and flakes easily with a fork.

4 servings.

CONNECTICUT STUFFED BAKED SHAD

Adriah David Smith
Oregon, Missouri

1 cup cracker crumbs

¼ cup melted butter

¼ teaspoon salt

¼ teaspoon freshly ground pepper

1 small onion, minced

1 teaspoon sage

1 large shad, head on, cleaned

1 cup hot water

¼ lb. bacon strips

❶ Heat oven to 400°F.

❷ In medium bowl, combine cracker crumbs, melted butter, salt, pepper, onion and sage. Stuff cracker-crumb mixture into fish; close and secure with toothpicks.

❸ Place fish on rack in large baking dish. Add water; lay strips of bacon on the fish. Bake 10 minutes, then reduce heat to 350°F. Bake an additional 35 minutes, basting frequently, until fish flakes easily with a fork.

6 servings.

SALMON WITH LEMON-CAPER BUTTER

SALMON WITH LEMON-CAPER BUTTER

John Anderson
Anderson, California

8 tablespoons butter

3 tablespoons fresh Italian parsley, minced

2 garlic cloves, minced

2 tablespoons capers, rinsed and drained

2 tablespoons grated lemon peel

1 teaspoon salt

¼ teaspoon freshly ground pepper

6 salmon steaks, cut ¾ to 1 inch thick

1 tablespoon extra-virgin olive oil

❶ Heat oven to 350°F.

❷ In medium bowl, beat butter with an electric mixer until soft. Add parsley, garlic, capers, lemon peel, ¾ teaspoon of the salt and ⅛ teaspoon of the pepper; beat to combine. Set lemon-caper butter aside and chill.

❸ Brush salmon with olive oil and season with remaining ¼ teaspoon salt and ⅛ teaspoon pepper. Bake until just opaque throughout, 15 to 18 minutes depending on thickness of steaks. Serve hot fish with cold lemon-caper butter.

6 servings.

BAKED CRAPPIE ALMONDINE

Frank V. Jovenall
Sharpsville, Pennsylvania

1 lb. crappie fillets

1 teaspoon grated lemon peel

2 tablespoons vegetable oil

2 tablespoons lemon juice

2 teaspoons chopped parsley

Salt to taste

Freshly ground pepper to taste

½ cup slivered almonds

❶ Heat oven to 350°F. Spray large baking dish with nonstick cooking spray.

❷ Place fillets in single layer in prepared baking dish.

❸ In medium bowl, mix together lemon peel, vegetable oil, lemon juice, parsley, salt and pepper; beat until blended. Spread mixture evenly over fish, then sprinkle with almonds. Bake 30 minutes or until fish flakes at thickest end with fork.

2 servings.

EMILIE'S BAKED FILLETS

Robert Delcourt
Gatineau, Quebec, Canada

1 (2-lb.) center-cut salmon fillet

1 tablespoon extra-virgin olive oil

¼ teaspoon Mrs. Dash

¼ teaspoon turmeric

¼ teaspoon parsley

❶ Heat oven to 350°F.

❷ Coat fillet with olive oil and place on a baking sheet. Sprinkle with Mrs. Dash, turmeric and parsley. Bake 30 minutes or until fish flakes easily with a fork. Serve on a bed of rice or salad, and sprinkle fish with lemon juice.

4 servings.

BAKED WALLEYE FILLETS

Thomas Lang
Houston, Pennsylvania

1 cup sour cream

1 tablespoon horseradish

1 cup fine bread crumbs

½ cup Parmesan cheese

1 teaspoon oregano

1 teaspoon basil

1 teaspoon parsley

1 teaspoon salt

¼ teaspoon freshly ground pepper

2 lbs. walleye fillets, cut into 4 pieces

❶ Heat oven to 400°F.

❷ In medium bowl, mix sour cream and horseradish.

❸ In a separate medium bowl, combine bread crumbs, Parmesan cheese, oregano, basil, parsley, salt and pepper. Spread sour cream mixture evenly over fillets, then coat well with bread crumb mixture.

❹ Place fillets on baking sheet and bake 10 minutes per side or until fish flakes easily with a fork.

4 servings.

BAKED COHO SALMON

Gerald Kuehn
Wautoma, Wisconsin

FISH

1 (4½- to 5-lb.) Coho salmon, cleaned and dressed

6 tablespoons lemon juice

Seasoned salt to taste

2 lemons, sliced

2 onions, sliced

4 bay leaves

⅓ cup butter, melted

Fresh parsley to taste

TARTAR SAUCE

2 tablespoons capers

2 tablespoons chopped pickle

2 tablespoons minced olives

1 tablespoon minced parsley

1 teaspoon grated onion

2 cups mayonnaise

❶ Heat oven to 350°F.

❷ For Fish: Brush inside of fish with about 2 tablespoons of the lemon juice, then sprinkle with seasoned salt. Stuff fish loosely with lemon slices, onion slices and bay leaves. Combine remaining lemon juice with melted butter and brush over skin of fish. Sprinkle with additional seasoned salt. Set on rack in shallow pan and cover tail with aluminum foil to prevent burning. Bake about 1½ hours or until fish flakes easily with a fork. Baste fish with lemon butter every 15 to 20 minutes. When done, remove onions, lemon and bay leaves; discard. Uncover tail. Garnish with additional lemon slices and parsley.

❸ For Tartar Sauce: In medium bowl, combine capers, pickle, olives, parsley, onion and mayonnaise; mix well. Yields 2½ cups.

10 servings.

WALLEYE, GMFC STYLE

David Wittwer
Madison, Wisconsin

4 tablespoons butter

3 tablespoons olive oil

1 small onion, chopped

1 small zucchini, chopped

½ cup fresh mushrooms, chopped

½ lb. sea scallops, chopped

½ lb. small peeled and deveined shrimp, chopped

1½ teaspoons Old Bay seasoning

1¾ cups crushed Ritz crackers

Salt to taste

Freshly ground pepper to taste

2 tablespoons butter, melted

8 to 10 walleye fillets (approximately 2 lbs. total)

❶ In large skillet, heat butter and oil over medium-high heat. Add onion, zucchini and mushrooms; cook, stirring often, until vegetables are softened and lightly browned, about 6 minutes. Add scallops, shrimp and seasoning; cook, stirring often, until seafood is just cooked through, about 3 to 4 minutes. Remove from heat. Add cracker crumbs. Season with salt and pepper.

❷ Heat oven to 400°F. Brush 13x9-inch glass baking dish generously with melted butter. Season fillets on both sides with salt and pepper. Arrange 4 or 5 of the fillets in the baking dish. Cover with stuffing, pressing it in to make an even layer, and top with the remaining fillets. Brush the fish with melted butter. Bake about 20 to 30 minutes or until fish is opaque and flakes easily with a fork.

4 to 6 servings.

BAKED FISHERMAN'S STEAK

A. Cordell Jones
Philadelphia, Pennsylvania

6 salmon steaks, 1 inch thick

½ cup Miracle Whip salad dressing

2 tablespoons sweet pickle relish

2 tablespoons parsley, chopped

2 egg whites

Lemon slices

❶ Heat oven to 350°F. Spray large, glass baking dish with nonstick cooking spray.

❷ Place fish steaks in prepared baking dish and bake 20 minutes. Remove fish steaks from oven.

❸ In large bowl, combine salad dressing, pickle relish and parsley. In small bowl, beat egg whites until stiff peaks form; fold into salad dressing mixture. Spread mixture evenly over steaks.

❹ Increase oven to 400°F. Place fish steaks in baking dish and bake 10 minutes or until fish flakes easily with a fork. Garnish with lemon slices.

6 servings.

BAKED STUFFED FISH

Leslie Richardson
San Benito, TX

1 (6- to 7-lb.) fish, cleaned and deboned (striped bass, red snapper, redfish, large mackerel, haddock, bluefish or salmon)

2 tablespoons oil

1 small onion, finely chopped

Minced fresh garlic to taste

Celery, finely chopped

1 cup cooked brown rice

1 tablespoon parsley, chopped

1 tablespoon Worcestershire sauce

1/4 cup slivered almonds

1/2 teaspoon salt

1/2 teaspoon freshly ground pepper

1 tablespoon all-purpose flour, seasoned with salt and pepper

1/2 cup white wine

❶ Heat oven to 400°F.

❷ Place fish in a large, lightly-oiled glass or enamel baking dish that can be used for serving.

❸ In large skillet, heat oil over medium-high heat until hot. Add onion; cook until onion is just limp. Add garlic; cook 2 to 3 minutes. Remove skillet from heat. Add celery, rice, parsley, Worcestershire sauce and almonds; toss lightly. Season with salt and pepper.

❹ Stuff fish with onion mixture; close and secure with toothpicks. Rub seasoned flour over the top of the fish. Cut three crosswise slashes in the skin at equal intervals. This will help the fish to keep its shape while baking. Pour wine around the fish.

❺ Bake uncovered 15 minutes. Reduce heat to 375°F and bake an additional 35 minutes or until fish flakes easily with a fork. Baste a few times with pan juices.

6 to 7 servings.

TOMMY'S BAKED TROUT

T. E. Grainger
Corona, California

2 tablespoons fresh basil, chopped

2 tablespoons fresh mint, chopped

2 tablespoons fresh thyme, chopped

2 tablespoons fresh rosemary, chopped

2 tablespoons fresh garlic, chopped

4 (8 to 10 oz. each) trout

1/2 cup Pinot Grigio white wine

1/3 cup extra-virgin olive oil

❶ Heat oven to 325°F.

❷ In medium bowl, combine basil, mint, thyme, rosemary and garlic; mix together well.

❸ Lay trout in baking dish. Stuff basil mixture evenly into each cavity and on top of each trout. Pour wine and olive oil evenly over each fish. Cover baking pan with aluminum foil and bake 35 to 40 minutes or until fish flakes easily with a fork. Serve with a favorite vegetable and/or rice dish and chilled wine.

4 servings.

TOMMY'S BAKED TROUT

Smoked, Pickled & Preserved

ROGER'S SMOKED SALMON

Bill Brown
Juneau, Alaska

BRINE

1 quart water

1 cup apple or cherry juice

1½ cups packed brown sugar

3 cups non-iodized salt

6 garlic cloves, crushed

15 whole cloves

1 teaspoon crushed red pepper

FISH

4 lbs. salmon (King, Coho, Sockeye or Chum)

❶ In glass or plastic container, mix brine until salt and sugar are dissolved. Cut salmon into ¼-pound pieces (leave skin on) and submerge completely in brine. Cover container and place brine overnight in refrigerator. In the morning, remove salmon and rinse in cold water. Pat dry with paper towels and place on racks, skin-side down. Allow to air dry 2 hours or until salmon is slightly tacky.

❷ For smoking: Use a mixture of alder and hickory chips in an electric Big Chief smoker. Smoke according to manufacturer's directions. Salmon should be cooked to 160°F for at least 30 minutes.

3 pounds.

HAWAIIAN JALAPEÑO POKE

Earl Okuda
Salt Lake City, UT

1 lb. sushi grade tuna

½ sliced sweet onion

1 green onion, finely chopped

4 jalapeño peppers, seeded and sliced

¼ cup soy sauce

2 tablespoons sesame oil

1 teaspoon sea salt

❶ Cut raw tuna into 1-inch cubes and place in large bowl. Add sweet onion, green onion, jalapeño, soy sauce and sesame oil. Chill. Before serving, add sea salt.

4 servings.

SMOKED FISH OMELET

Bill Burpo
Holcombe, Wisconsin

3 eggs

2 tablespoons milk

⅛ teaspoon freshly ground pepper

1 tablespoon margarine or butter

½ cup flaked smoked fish

¼ cup shredded cheddar or Swiss cheese

❶ In small bowl, blend eggs, milk and pepper.

❷ In medium skillet, melt margarine over medium heat. Pour eggs into skillet and cook until eggs are set, about 5 minutes. Sprinkle fish and cheese over half of omelet. With spatula, carefully fold other half over filling. Cook until cheese melts, about 1 to 2 minutes.

2 servings.

HAWAIIAN JALAPEÑO POKE

TEA-SMOKED SALMON WITH WASABI CUCUMBER REMOULADE

TEA-SMOKED SALMON WITH WASABI CUCUMBER REMOULADE

Michael Pettipiece
San Jose, California

BRINE

5 cups water

1 cup sake

1/2 cup sugar

1/2 cup kosher (coarse) salt

2 tablespoons minced fresh ginger

1 tablespoon toasted whole Szechwan peppercorns

1 side skinless salmon fillet (5 to 6 lbs.), pin bones
    removed

REMOULADE

6 tablespoons pommery mustard

2 tablespoons wasabi paste

1 tablespoon chopped garlic

1/3 cup rice wine vinegar

2/3 cup canola oil

1/3 cup chopped cucumbers, peeled and seeded

1/3 cup chopped scallions, green parts only

2 tablespoons chopped cilantro

Salt to taste

Freshly ground pepper to taste

SMOKING MIX

2 cups sugar

2 cups long grain rice

2 cups jasmine tea

❶ For Brine: In medium bowl, combine water, sake, sugar, salt, ginger and peppercorns. Stir until salt and sugar have dissolved. Place fish in salmon poacher. Pour liquid over salmon; cover and allow to brine, refrigerated, at least 2 hours. Remove fish from poacher; allow to dry at least 2 hours.

❷ For Remoulade: In food processor, combine mustard, wasabi paste, garlic and vinegar. While the processor is running, slowly drizzle in the canola oil until an emulsion is formed. Remove mayonnaise-like mixture from processor and place in a non-reactive stainless-steel bowl. Fold in cucumbers, scallions and cilantro. Season with salt and pepper. Refrigerate until ready to use.

❸ Clean poacher. Place 2 overturned ramekins on either side of the inside of the poacher. Line interior of poacher up to the rim with foil, making sure foil is placed over ramekins. Repeat with another piece of foil. Add sugar, rice and jasmine tea to foil-lined poacher; cover and heat over medium heat until rice mixture begins to smoke. Place salmon on top of poaching rack, lower into the poacher. Reduce heat to low and smoke salmon, covered, 15 minutes. Turn off heat and smoke salmon an additional 15 minutes. (Salmon should be cooked to 160°F for at least 30 minutes.) Garnish with 1 medium peeled cucumber and thinly sliced toast points.

8 servings.

FISH JERKY

Tyler Newman
Holt, Missouri

FISH

2 lbs. favorite fish, cut into 3x1-inch strips,
    1/4 inch thick

MARINADE

1/2 cup Worcestershire sauce

1/2 cup soy sauce

2 tablespoons sugar

2 tablespoons ketchup

4 teaspoons salt

1/2 teaspoon onion powder

1/2 teaspoon freshly ground pepper

1 garlic clove, crushed

❶ In large bowl, stir together Worcestershire sauce, soy sauce, sugar, ketchup, salt, onion powder, pepper and garlic. Add fish. Cover and refrigerate 1 to 2 hours.

❷ Remove fish from marinade; discard marinade. Place fish in dehydrator. Follow manufacturer's directions.

2 pounds jerky.

BEER DRINKER'S BRINE FOR FISH

Richard Hansen
Burlington, Ontario, Canada

BRINE
1 cup non-iodized salt

1 cup packed brown sugar

1 cup soy sauce

½ cup cider vinegar

1 tablespoon Worcestershire sauce

1 tablespoon onion powder

1 tablespoon garlic powder

½ tablespoon freshly ground pepper

1 tablespoon paprika

1 tablespoon chili powder

3 cups water

FISH
Cooked fish chunks, filets or small whole fish

❶ For Brine: In large container, combine salt, brown sugar, soy sauce, cider vinegar, Worcestershire sauce, onion powder, garlic powder, pepper, paprika, chili powder and water; mix thoroughly until well dissolved. Immerse fish in brine; refrigerate. (Brine fish 1 inch thick 5 to 8 hours; fish ½ inch thick 4 hours; and thinner fillets or pieces 2 to 3 hours.)

❷ Remove fish from brine; discard brine. Rinse fish thoroughly; pat dry and allow to air dry about 1 hour. This will cause a "pellicle" (a tacky glaze on the fish) to form indicating it is ready for the drying and smoking process.

❸ Try using hickory or mesquite wood chips with this brine when smoking fish. Smoke according to manufacturer's directions.

Servings vary.

TEXAS SMOKED FLOUNDER

Andrew J. Krotje
Brooksville, Florida

1 whole flounder (about 4 lbs.), cleaned

1 lemon, halved

1 tablespoon olive oil

½ teaspoon freshly ground pepper

2 tablespoons chopped fresh dill

1 cup wood chips, soaked

❶ Heat smoker for high heat, about 350°F (175°C).

❷ With sharp knife, cut 3 or 4 diagonal slits on fish body big enough for lemon slices. Slice half of the lemon into thin slices. Rub a light coating of olive oil over fish; then squeeze remaining lemon half over fish. Rub in pepper. Press 1 tablespoon of the dill into slits; insert lemon slices firmly.

❸ Place flounder on large piece of aluminum foil; fold sides up high around fish. There should be enough foil to seal into a packet, although you want it open for now. Place fish on smoker and throw a couple of handfuls of soaked wood chips onto coals. Close lid and smoke until fish flakes easily with a fork. Garnish with remaining fresh dill. Refrigerate up to 2 weeks or freeze.

Serves 8.

PICKLED FISH

Tanya Orth
Chaska, Minnesota

4 pints fish fillets

1 cup salt

4 cups water

2 cups white vinegar

1¼ cups sugar

2 teaspoons mustard seed

4 bay leaves

5 whole cloves

1 teaspoon whole allspice

1 teaspoon whole black pepper

1 onion, sliced

❶ Cut fish crosswise into ½-inch strips.

❷ In large bowl, mix salt and water. Soak fish in saltwater solution in refrigerator 48 hours. Drain and rinse pieces well in cold water. Place fish back in bowl and cover with white vinegar 24 hours. Take fish out of bowl and drain. Do not rinse.

❸ For brine, combine 2 cups white vinegar, sugar, mustard seed, bay leaves, cloves, allspice and pepper in large saucepan; bring to a boil and place in refrigerator until cool. Place fish, plus a generous amount of onion slices, in wide-mouth gallon jar. Pour brine over fish, cover jar and refrigerate 2 weeks.

Servings vary.

SMOKED FISH ON A KETTLE-TYPE GRILL

Daniel Clark
Austin, Minnesota

4 lbs. salmon or trout

1 cup canning and pickling salt

½ gallon fresh water

❶ Use fire shield 1 inch below the grate with a 1-inch gap around edge to allow smoke through. Cut wood into 1-inch cubes; soak in water at least an hour if using dead and dried wood. (Green wood does not need the water soaking.)

❷ In large container, combine salt and water; stir until completely dissolved. Soak fish in brine in refrigerator at least 8 hours.

❸ Start charcoal using enough for a single layer of coals. When charcoal is ready, place handful of wood chunks on top of coals. Place grate over coals with fire shield in place.

❹ Remove fish from brine; discard brine. Place fish on grate in single layer, leaving a little room between pieces. Cover grill, venting slightly. Salmon should be cooked to 160°F for at least 30 minutes.

3 pounds.

MOM'S PICKLED PIKE

Richard Hansen
Burlington, Ontario, Canada

BRINE

1½ cups salt

1 gallon water

FISH

6 lbs. pike fillets, cut into 2-inch chunks

4 cups distilled white vinegar

8 bay leaves

2 teaspoons whole cloves

2 teaspoons whole black pepper

2½ cups sugar

4 teaspoons mustard seed

2 teaspoons whole allspice

Onions, sliced

❶ In large container, combine salt and water. Immerse fish in brine 2 days. Store in refrigerator. Remove fish from brine; discard brine. Soak fish in vinegar. Refrigerate 7 to 10 days, stirring every couple days.

❷ Remove fish from vinegar. In large saucepan, bring vinegar, bay leaves, cloves, pepper, sugar, mustard seed, allspice and onions to a boil over medium heat. Boil 10 minutes, then cool.

❸ Pack fish into pint jars, alternating layers of fish with onion. Pour spiced vinegar mix over fish; refrigerate an additional 2 days.

Servings vary.

SMOKED SALMON

Larry Six
Puyallup, Washington

1 (2-lb.) pkg. packed brown sugar

½ cup rock salt

4 lbs. salmon, skinned, filleted and cut into 1½-inch chunks

❶ Mix sugar and salt; spread thin layer in dish. Add layer of salmon; cover with sugar mix. Repeat with another layer of salmon. Repeat until all salmon and mix is used. Cover and store mixture in refrigerator 24 hours. During curing process, remove container several times to tilt or invert to thoroughly mix ingredients.

❷ Remove salmon from mixture; discard mixture. Rinse salmon thoroughly with cool water. Place salmon on cooling racks; pat dry with paper towels. Arrange salmon on baking sheets (uncovered); refrigerate an additional 8 to 10 hours.

❸ Smoke according to manufacturer's directions. Salmon should be cooked to 160°F for at least 30 minutes.

3 pounds.

SMOKED LAKE ERIE STEELHEAD SPREAD

SMOKED LAKE ERIE STEELHEAD SPREAD

Thomas Lang
Houston, Pennsylvania

1 lb. smoked steelhead, cleaned, flaked
8 oz. cream cheese, softened
1/2 cup sour cream
1/4 cup chopped capers
2 tablespoons finely chopped shallots
1 tablespoon chopped fresh dill

❶ In medium bowl, combine steelhead, cream cheese, sour cream, capers, shallots and fresh dill. Refrigerate at least 4 hours. Serve with toast points or crackers.

4 servings.

SMOKED FISH

Lavern Molzof
Montfort, Wisconsin

2 to 3 lbs. fish
1 pint pickling salt
1 pint brown sugar

❶ Mix equal parts pickling salt and brown sugar. Throw a handful or two of mixture into plastic bag and drop in a whole, dressed fish or fillets; turn to coat thoroughly. Add more mixture and more fish until all fish are generously coated. Close bag airtight and leave in cool place overnight. Fish will release enough moisture to create thick brine.

❷ Rinse fish in water to remove all salt and sugar from surface. Place on racks to dry until a "glaze" forms. Place fish on racks or rods and put in smoker. Proper smoking takes at least 6 hours. Smoke until fish is browned and flakes easily with a fork.

❸ Smoked fish can be kept in refrigerator for a month or so and can be packaged and frozen for several months.

Servings vary.

PICKLED FISH

Bruce Kitowski
Sartell, Minnesota

SALT BRINE
1 cup canning and pickling salt
1 quart water (4 cups)
1 cup white vinegar
4 lbs. fish, skinned and cut into 1-inch pieces

PICKLING BRINE
2 cups white vinegar
1 cup sugar
2 cups white wine
2 tablespoons pickling spice
1/2 cup water
1 cup chopped onion

❶ For Salt Brine: In large container, combine salt and water; stir until salt is dissolved. Immerse fish in salt brine 24 hours. Remove fish from brine; discard brine. Rinse fish thoroughly.

❷ In another large container, cover fish completely with white vinegar; let soak 24 hours. Remove fish from vinegar; discard vinegar.

❸ For Pickling Brine: In medium pot, combine fish, white vinegar, sugar, white wine, pickling spice and water; boil 15 minutes. Let cool until just warm. Pack fish in jars. Divide onion evenly between jars. Pour warm pickling brine over fish. Seal tight; let stand at room temperature 24 hours away from heat. Refrigerate 3 days before eating.

3 (1-quart) jars.

Broiled, Foiled
& Poached

BROILED TROUT DIJONNAISE

Frank V. Jovenall
Sharpsville, Pennsylvania

4 (about 8 oz. each) small trout

Salt to taste

2 tablespoons melted butter

1 tablespoon dry white wine

1 tablespoon Dijon mustard

¼ teaspoon dry tarragon

Lemon wedges

❶ Rinse trout inside and out; pat dry. Salt trout to taste. In small bowl, mix together butter, white wine, Dijon mustard and tarragon. Brush trout inside and out with half of the mixture. Place trout on broiler pan 4 inches from heat. Cook 5 minutes, then turn. Brush with remaining mixture. Return to broiler and cook about 4 minutes or until fish flakes easily with fork. Serve with lemon wedges.

4 servings.

BARBECUED CATFISH

William Biacco
Oakdale, Pennsylvania

¼ cup ketchup

2 tablespoons light (mild) molasses

2 teaspoons red wine vinegar

¼ teaspoon Worcestershire sauce

4 (about 6 oz. each) catfish fillets

❶ Preheat broiler.

❷ In small bowl combine ketchup, molasses, vinegar and Worcestershire sauce. Place catfish fillets, skin side up, on rack in broiling pan. Brush half of sauce on catfish. Place pan in broiler about 6 inches from heat; broil 4 minutes. Brush remaining sauce on fillets (do not turn), and broil until fish is opaque throughout and flakes easily with a fork, about an additional 4 minutes.

4 servings.

FILLET OF SOLE

John Anderson
Anderson, California

1 medium onion, chopped

3 garlic cloves, minced

Salt to taste

Freshly ground pepper to taste

2 tablespoons olive oil

1 tablespoon Italian parsley

1 tablespoon chopped fresh basil

1 large ripe tomato, peeled and chopped

1 lb. fillet of sole

Juice of ½ lemon

❶ In large, covered skillet, sauté onion, garlic, salt and pepper in olive oil until onion is opaque. Add parsley and basil; cook 1 minute, stirring constantly. Add tomato; cook, stirring gently, 10 minutes. Lay fillet of sole in skillet and spread mixture over fish. Add lemon juice and cover. Cook over medium heat 10 minutes or until fish flakes easily with fork. Serve fish over steamed rice.

4 servings.

MY FAVORITE SALMON

Donald Mower
Covelo, California

4 (5-oz.) salmon fillets

½ teaspoon salt

¼ teaspoon freshly ground pepper

2 teaspoons canola oil

¼ cup water

¼ cup balsamic vinegar (do not substitute)

4½ teaspoons lemon juice

1 tablespoon packed brown sugar

❶ Sprinkle both sides of fillets with salt and pepper.

❷ In large, nonstick skillet, cook salmon in oil over medium heat 10 to 15 minutes or until fish flakes easily with a fork, turning once. Remove and keep warm.

❸ In large bowl, combine water, vinegar, lemon juice and brown sugar; pour into skillet. Bring to a boil and cook until liquid is reduced to about ⅓ cup. Serve over salmon.

4 servings.

FILLET ITALIANO

Christian Noblitt
Indianapolis, Indiana

4 (6 to 8 oz. each) fish fillets

½ cup bread or cracker crumbs

2 tablespoons olive oil

2 tablespoons butter

1 sweet onion, thinly sliced

1 cup (4 oz.) grated mozzarella cheese

½ cup grated Parmesan cheese

¼ cup of your favorite balsamic vinaigrette dressing

❶ Heat oven to 350°F.

❷ Coat fish fillets with crumbs. In large skillet, heat olive oil and butter over medium-high heat until hot. Add fillets; cook 2 minutes per side or until brown. Remove fillets to ovenproof dish. Layer with sliced onions and cheese. Bake 20 to 25 minutes or until fish flakes easily with a fork. Drizzle with dressing.

4 servings.

STEELHEAD WITH GARLIC SAUCE

Frank V. Jovenall
Sharpsville, Pennsylvania

GARLIC SAUCE
1/3 cup butter, divided
12 garlic cloves, finely chopped

FISH
2 lbs. steelhead fillets
Salt to taste
Freshly ground pepper to taste
1 egg
1 tablespoon water
2 tablespoons vegetable oil
Lemon wedges

❶ For Garlic Sauce: In small frying pan, melt 3 tablespoons of the butter over medium-low heat. Add garlic, stirring occasionally about 8 to 15 minutes or until golden. Remove pan from heat and keep warm.

❷ Rinse fish thoroughly and pat dry. Season with salt and pepper. In shallow pie pan, beat egg and water.

❸ In large skillet, heat oil and remaining butter over medium heat until frothy. Dip each fillet in egg mixture. Fry, turning once, until fish flakes easily with a fork. Pour garlic sauce over fish and garnish with lemon wedges.

4 to 6 servings.

TOMATO-ORANGE FISH FILLETS

Steven C. Baker
Colorado Springs, Colorado

2 tablespoons extra-virgin olive oil
1/2 teaspoon dried thyme
1 (14.5-oz.) can petite diced tomatoes in juice
3/4 cup orange juice
4 fresh fish fillets, approximately 4 oz. each
Salt to taste
Freshly ground pepper to taste
2 teaspoons finely chopped fresh cilantro

❶ In large saucepan, cook oil and thyme over medium-high heat. Pour tomatoes with juice into saucepan. Add orange juice, stirring to combine thoroughly. Bring mixture to a simmer; cook uncovered approximately 10 to 15 minutes or until mixture thickens slightly. Season fish fillets with salt and pepper. Gently add fish fillets to tomato/orange mixture; cover and cook 3 minutes. Remove lid and cook until fish flakes easily with a fork and sauce has thickened.

❷ To serve, carefully remove a fish fillet from the pan and spoon about 1/4 of the tomato mixture over the fillet. Lightly sprinkle each fillet with 1/2 teaspoon chopped fresh cilantro.

4 servings.

TOMATO-ORANGE FISH FILLETS

CRISPY WHOLE STRIPED BASS WITH RED TOMATILLO SAUCE

CRISPY WHOLE STRIPED BASS WITH RED TOMATILLO SAUCE

John Seay
Las Vegas, Nevada

RED TOMATILLO SAUCE
8 tomatillos, husked and washed

4 tablespoons olive oil

1 large red onion, finely chopped

2 garlic cloves, finely chopped

1/2 habanero chile pepper, coarsely chopped

3 tablespoons New Mexico chili powder

1/4 cup red wine vinegar

2 tablespoons honey

3 tablespoons chopped fresh cilantro

Salt to taste

Freshly ground pepper to taste

FISH
Peanut or canola oil for frying

1 cup rice flour

Salt to taste

Freshly ground pepper to taste

1/2 cup water

2 whole striped bass, about 1 lb. each, cleaned, rinsed and patted dry

❶ For Tomatillo Sauce: Heat oven to 375°F. Place tomatillos in small roasting pan; toss with 2 tablespoons of the olive oil and season with salt and pepper. Roast until soft, about 20 to 25 minutes. Heat remaining 2 tablespoons oil in skillet. Add onions; cook until soft. Add garlic and habanero and cook 1 minute. Add chili powder and cook an additional 1 minute. Stir in tomatillos and cook 10 minutes. Transfer mixture to food processor. Add vinegar, honey and cilantro; process until almost smooth. Season with salt and pepper.

❷ For Fish: Heat about 2 inches of oil in high-sided, heavy skillet over medium heat to 360°F. In large bowl, whisk together flour, salt and pepper. Whisk in enough water to make batter the consistency of crepe batter. Season fish with salt and pepper inside and out; then dip into batter allowing any excess to run off. Carefully place fish in oil; fry until golden brown on both sides and fish flakes easily with a fork. Place each fish on a large plate; ladle with red tomatillo sauce.

4 servings.

SAUTÉED WHITEFISH WITH ROSEMARY, GARLIC AND SAGE

Dennis Reynolds
Billings, Montana

1/2 cup all-purpose flour

2 tablespoons rubbed sage

2 tablespoons fresh chopped rosemary

1/2 teaspoon salt

1/4 teaspoon freshly ground pepper

3 tablespoons olive oil

4 (6 to 8 oz. each) whitefish fillets

2 tablespoons butter

2 garlic cloves, finely chopped

❶ In medium bowl, combine flour, sage, rosemary, salt and pepper. Dust fillets with seasoned flour mixture.

❷ Heat 1 tablespoon of the olive oil in large skillet over medium-high heat. Add fillets; cook until outside is browned and fish flakes easily with a fork, about 1 or 2 minutes per side. Remove to warming plate and reduce heat to medium. Add butter, remaining 2 tablespoons olive oil and garlic; cook until garlic softens, about 4 minutes. Serve with lemon wedges.

4 servings.

RAYSTOWN BASS FILLETS

Charles L. Troutman
Glendale, Arizona

1½ to 2 lbs. bass fillets

Salt to taste

Freshly ground pepper to taste

¼ cup butter, melted

1 tablespoon lemon juice

¼ teaspoon grated lemon peel

¼ teaspoon grated orange peel

1 teaspoon dried tarragon

❶ Season fillets with salt and pepper. In large bowl, combine butter, lemon juice, lemon peel, orange peel and tarragon. Butter aluminum foil and place on broiler pan. Place fillets on foil. Brush a little of the butter mixture evenly over the fillets. Broil approximately 4 inches from heat, brushing fillets often with butter mixture, about 8 to 10 minutes or until fish flakes easily with a fork. Garnish with parsley sprigs, and lemon or lime wedges as desired.

4 servings.

POACHED CATFISH IN GINGER SAUCE

Michael Bunker
New Lisbon, Wisconsin

2 tablespoons peanut or vegetable oil

1 garlic clove, minced

5 tablespoons fresh ginger, peeled and very finely minced or grated

½ cup chicken, beef or vegetable broth or water

¼ cup soy sauce

¼ cup dry white wine or water

1½ lbs. (8 to 10 oz. each) catfish or other fillets

Salt to taste

Freshly ground pepper to taste

❶ In large, deep skillet heat oil over medium heat until hot. Add garlic and 4 tablespoons of the ginger; stir once. When garlic begins to color, add broth, soy sauce and wine. Increase heat to high; reduce liquid by half. Season fillets with salt and pepper. Add fillets to liquid; cover and reduce heat to medium. Poach until fillets are white and opaque throughout, about 5 minutes. Garnish with reserved ginger. Serve over white rice.

4 servings.

ALBIE'S BUNDLES

Albert G. Phillips II
Milwaukee, Wisconsin

4 (4 to 5 oz. each) walleye, sole or panfish fillets

12 asparagus spears, trimmed

1 cup dry white wine

2 tablespoons chopped fresh mint

Salt to taste

Freshly ground pepper to taste

❶ Wrap each fillet around 3 asparagus spears. Place in 10-inch skillet. Pour white wine over roll-ups. Cook over medium-high heat until fish flakes easily with a fork. Sprinkle with mint. Season with salt and pepper.

4 servings.

BUTTERFISH WITH APPLES

Anita Karl
Cheyenne, Wyoming

FISH

2 medium apples, cored and cut into thin wedges

3 tablespoons butter

8 (6 to 8 oz. each) scaled drawn butterfish or
    4 (8 to 12 oz. each) scaled drawn porgies or
    rainbow trout

2 cups apple juice or apple cider

SAUCE

4 green onions, thinly sliced

1 tablespoon all-purpose flour

1/2 cup milk

1 tablespoon Dijon-style mustard

1 tablespoon chopped fresh parsley

❶ For Fish: In medium skillet, cook apples in 2 tablespoons of the butter over medium-high heat, about 1 minute or until lightly browned, turning once. Remove from heat. Place fish in baking dish large enough to hold them in a single layer. Add apples. Pour in enough apple juice or cider to half-cover the fish. Cover with foil. Bake at 350°F until fish flakes easily with a fork (about 20 minutes for butterfish, about 30 minutes for porgies or trout). Transfer fish and apples to a platter, reserving 1/4 cup of the liquid. Cover fish and apples to keep them warm while preparing the sauce.

❷ For Sauce: In small saucepan, cook onion in remaining 1 tablespoon of the butter until tender but not brown. Stir in flour. Add reserved liquid, milk and mustard. Cook and stir over medium heat until thickened and bubbly. Cook and stir an additional 1 minute. Stir in parsley. Pass sauce with fish.

4 servings.

LEMONADE-POACHED SALMON

Michael C. Gammino
San Jose, California

1 cup mayonnaise or tartar sauce

1 (12-oz.) can frozen lemonade concentrate, thawed

1/2 teaspoon freshly ground pepper

1/4 teaspoon crushed red pepper

1/4 cup water

1 1/2 lbs. center cut salmon fillet, cut into 4 pieces

❶ In medium bowl, combine mayonnaise or tartar sauce, 3 tablespoons of the lemonade concentrate, black pepper and red pepper; mix well, then cover and chill.

❷ In large skillet, combine remaining lemonade concentrate and water. Bring to a boil over medium-low heat. Add salmon, skin-side down, and reduce heat to low; cover and cook 12 minutes or until fish flakes easily with a fork. Allow salmon to cool to room temperature. Serve with the chilled lemonade sauce.

4 servings.

ITALIAN STYLE FILLETS

John Sikking
Lakeland, Florida

2 (8 to10 oz. each) fish fillets, cleaned

1 (16-oz.) bottle Italian dressing

1/4 cup butter, melted

2 Key limes

1/4 cup (2 oz.) provolone or mozzarella cheese, grated

1/4 cup chopped chives

Freshly ground pepper

1/4 cup chopped fresh parsley

Key lime peel, grated

❶ Heat oven to 350°F.

❷ In large, resealable plastic bag, marinate fillets in Italian dressing 30 minutes. Remove fillets from marinade; discard marinade.

❸ Place fillets in glass baking dish. Baste lightly with butter. Squeeze 1 Key lime evenly over fillets. Bake 3 to 4 minutes. Remove from heat; baste with additional butter. Sprinkle with cheese, chives, pepper, parsley and grated peel. Continue cooking until fish flakes easily with a fork. Drizzle with remaining Key lime juice. Serve hot.

2 servings.

BILLY JACK'S CURRIED TROUT

Bill Arcebal
Valdese, North Carolina

1 cup sweet yellow onions, sliced

4 garlic cloves, minced

1/2 cup tomatoes, diced

2 tablespoons olive oil

2 teaspoons curry powder

2 tablespoons fish sauce (available at Asian stores)

1 (14-oz.) can coconut milk

1/2 cup water

8 new potatoes, cut into 1/2-inch pieces

4 (6 to 8 oz. each) trout fillets, cut into bite-size pieces

1/2 teaspoon salt

❶ In medium saucepan, sauté onions, garlic, and tomatoes in oil 3 minutes. Add curry powder and fish sauce while stirring. Add milk and water; simmer 3 minutes. Add potatoes and trout; cook 15 minutes or until potatoes are tender and fish flakes easily with a fork. Season with fish sauce to taste. Serve over cooked rice.

4 servings.

BILLY JACK'S CURRIED TROUT

SOUTHWEST STYLE FILLETS

John Sikking
Lakeland, Florida

2 (8 to 10 oz. each) fish fillets, skin removed and
    deboned (mahi-mahi, grouper, snapper, bass or
    speckled perch)
2 tablespoons olive oil
1 (1.25-oz) pkg. dry taco seasoning mix
¼ cup chopped fresh chives

❶ Heat oven to 350°F.

❷ Drizzle fillets evenly with olive oil and place in
large, resealable plastic bag. Add package of taco
seasoning; shake until fillets are coated evenly.
Remove fillets from plastic bag; discard seasoning.
Place fillets in glass baking dish and sprinkle with
chives. Bake until fish flakes easily with a fork.
Remove from heat and serve hot.

2 servings.

BROILED SALMON STEAK

Victor Toledo
New York, New York

1 (1-lb.) salmon steak, center bone removed
Salt to taste
Freshly ground pepper to taste
1 (1-inch) piece fresh ginger, minced
2 medium garlic cloves, minced
2 teaspoons soy sauce
2 tablespoons butter
2 tablespoons dry white wine

❶ Heat oven to 350°F. Lightly oil broiler pan.

❷ Remove spine of steak leaving two slender fillets.
Place fillets, skin side down, on prepared broiler pan.
Season with salt and pepper. Sprinkle ginger and
garlic on fillets. Coat fillets with soy sauce. Put pats
of butter on top of fish. Place under broiler about
3 inches from heat. Broil 3 to 4 minutes. Remove pan
from broiler and pour wine over fillets. Bake about
2 to 2½ minutes for medium and 3 to 3½ minutes
for well done. Serve with rice, green vegetable salad
and broccoli or green beans. Pour juices over fish.

2 servings.

CAPTAIN JOHN'S FAVORITE ALASKAN HALIBUT

Captain John Ostdiek
Jordan, Minnesota

1 lb. halibut steaks
½ teaspoon salt
1 cup sliced fresh mushrooms
1 tablespoon butter
½ cup sour cream
1 tablespoon dry sherry
Paprika

❶ Heat oven to 425°F. Spray large baking dish with
nonstick cooking spray.

❷ Sprinkle halibut with salt. Place in prepared
baking dish. Bake 5 minutes. In medium saucepan,
sauté mushrooms in butter until tender. Remove
from heat; add sour cream and sherry. Spoon
mixture evenly over halibut. Sprinkle with paprika.

❸ Reduce oven temperature to 375°F. Continue
baking 20 minutes or until halibut flakes easily
with a fork.

4 servings.

POACHED FISH WITH HOLLANDAISE SAUCE

Gerald Kuehn
Wautoma, Wisconsin

COURT BOUILLON

2 cups water

1 carrot, sliced

1 rib celery, sliced

1 small onion, sliced

1 lemon, sliced

4 peppercorns

2 bay leaves

2 parsley sprigs

1 teaspoon salt

POACHED FISH

4 (8 to 10 oz. each) fish fillets, cut into 1-inch pieces

Court bouillon

Easy Hollandaise Sauce

Chopped parsley

Lemon wedges

EASY HOLLANDAISE SAUCE

1/4 cup melted butter

1 tablespoon all-purpose flour

1/4 teaspoon salt

1/8 teaspoon white pepper

Dash of cayenne pepper

1 cup milk

1 egg yolk, lightly beaten

1 tablespoon lemon juice

❶ For Bouillon: In medium saucepan, bring water to a boil. Add carrot, celery, onion, lemon, peppercorns, bay leaves, parsley and salt. Cover and simmer 10 minutes. With slotted spoon remove vegetables, lemon and spices; discard. Yields about 2 cups.

❷ For Poached Fish: Place fillet pieces in court bouillon. Cover and simmer 7 to 8 minutes or until fish flakes easily with a fork. With slotted spoon carefully remove fish to serving platter. Meanwhile, prepare Hollandaise Sauce: Melt butter in small saucepan. Add flour, salt, white pepper and cayenne pepper; blend. Add milk gradually, stirring until thickened. Add egg yolk; mix and cook about

1 minute, stirring constantly. Remove from heat. Add lemon juice gradually and beat vigorously. Yields about 1 1/3 cups. Pour hollandaise sauce evenly over fillets. Garnish with chopped parsley and lemon wedges.

6 servings.

GRILLED CATFISH WITH FRESH SALSA

Brian Balmat
Blue Springs, Missouri

SALSA

3 medium tomatoes, chopped

1/4 cup chopped onion

2 medium jalapeño peppers, chopped

3 tablespoons white wine vinegar

1 teaspoon salt

FISH

4 catfish fillets

1/2 teaspoon garlic salt

1/2 teaspoon freshly ground pepper

1 teaspoon cayenne pepper

❶ In medium bowl, stir together tomatoes, onion, jalapeño peppers, vinegar and salt. Let stand at room temperature 30 minutes before serving.

❷ Meanwhile, prepare grill or preheat broiler. Sprinkle catfish fillets with garlic salt and peppers. Place fillets on oiled grill rack or broiler pan rack. Grill or broil about 4 inches from heat about 5 minutes on each side or until fish flakes easily with a fork. Place a fillet on each serving plate and spoon some Fresh Salsa over it.

4 servings.

BROILED TUNA STEAKS

Lawrence J. Hernandez
Merced, California

FISH

½ cup melted butter

½ teaspoon salt

1 tablespoon prepared mustard

2 teaspoons lemon juice

¼ teaspoon freshly ground pepper

4 tuna steaks (6 to 8 oz. each, 1 inch thick)

AVOCADO SAUCE

1 small ripe avocado, peeled and pitted

⅓ cup sour cream

1 teaspoon lemon juice

¼ teaspoon salt

Few drops Tabasco sauce

❶ For Fish: In medium bowl, combine butter, salt, mustard, lemon juice and pepper. Lightly grease broiler pan. Broil steaks 4 to 6 inches from heat on prepared broiler pan 5 to 8 minutes on each side or until fish flakes easily with a fork. Baste frequently with butter mixture.

❷ Meanwhile, in blender, mix together avocado, sour cream, lemon juice, salt and Tabasco until smooth. Serve with fish.

4 servings.

HALIBUT FISH BOIL

Dick Deno
Black River Falls, Wisconsin

Water to cover

12 small red potatoes

12 baby carrots

12 boiling onions

2 quarts water

¼ cup salt

¼ cup sugar

1½ lbs. halibut fillets, cut into 12 pieces

½ cup chopped fresh parsley

½ cup melted butter

❶ In 2-quart saucepan, cover potatoes, carrots and onions with water. Bring to a boil and cook 10 minutes or until tender. Meanwhile, in Dutch oven, mix 2 quarts water with salt and sugar. Bring to a boil; add halibut. Boil until fish flakes easily with a fork, about 3 to 4 minutes. Serve boiled vegetables with fish. Sprinkle with parsley. Serve with melted butter.

4 servings.

Grilled

CEDAR PLANK BASS

John T. Liles
Shreveport, Louisiana

2 bass fillets, about 1 lb.

2 tablespoons olive oil

1 teaspoon salt

½ teaspoon cayenne pepper

½ teaspoon freshly ground pepper

Emeril's Essence (creole seasoning), to taste

3 garlic cloves, finely chopped

2 ribs celery, chopped

3 green onions with tops, chopped

1 cup chopped green bell pepper

1 cup chopped red bell pepper

½ cup chopped mushrooms

1 Soak cedar plank in water 1 to 1½ hours. Heat oven to 350°F or heat grill. Place fillets in bowl and rub with 1 tablespoon of the olive oil; season with half of the spices. Place chopped vegetables and mushrooms in bowl; season with remaining 1 table-spoon olive oil and remaining spices. Stir until mixed well; set aside.

2 Remove soaked cedar plank from water and pat excess water from surface. Place fillets on plank; place vegetables on top of and around fillets. Bake or grill on medium heat 30 minutes or until fish flakes easily with a fork.

2 to 4 servings.

GRILLED SWORDFISH WITH ROSEMARY

Andrew J. Krotje
Brooksville, Florida

½ cup white wine

5 garlic cloves, minced

2 teaspoons chopped fresh rosemary

4 (4 oz. each) swordfish steaks

¼ teaspoon salt

¼ teaspoon freshly ground pepper

2 tablespoons lemon juice

1 tablespoon extra-virgin olive oil

4 slices lemon

1 Stir wine, garlic and 1 teaspoon of the rosemary together in 8-inch square baking dish. Sprinkle fish with salt and pepper. Place fish in baking dish, turning to coat. Cover and refrigerate at least 1 hour.

2 In small bowl, stir together the lemon juice, olive oil and remaining teaspoon of rosemary; set aside.

3 Heat grill. Transfer fish to a paper-towel-lined dish; discard marinade. Lightly oil grill grate. Grill fish 10 minutes over medium heat, turning once, or until fish flakes easily with a fork. Remove fish to serving plate. Spoon lemon sauce over fish, and top each fillet with a slice of lemon.

4 servings.

GRILLED SWORDFISH WITH ROSEMARY

ORANGE GLAZED SALMON

John Beason
Jonesboro, Arizona

Heavy-duty aluminum foil

1 (2- to 3-lb.) salmon fillet

2 to 4 tablespoons olive oil

1 to 2 teaspoons coarse sea salt

1 to 2 teaspoons freshly ground pepper

6 to 8 thyme sprigs

Thin slices lemon, lime, orange or tomato

1/2 cup frozen orange juice concentrate

1/2 cup molasses

❶ Heat grill. Fold aluminum foil to contain salmon fillet. Drizzle with olive oil, sprinkle with salt and pepper and top with half of the thyme sprigs. Place foil plate on grill; place salmon on foil. Season with remaining oil, salt, pepper and thyme. Place lemon slices on salmon.

❷ In small bowl, combine orange juice and molasses.

❸ Cook fillet 15 to 20 minutes or until fish flakes easily with a fork, basting with orange and molasses mixture.

6 servings.

CAMPFIRE GRILLED SALMON OR TROUT

Charles Troccia
Keene, New Hampshire

2 (6 to 8 oz. each) salmon or trout fillets, skin removed

1/4 cup mayonnaise or to taste

1 tablespoon Old Bay seasoning

6 slices of cob or apple-smoked bacon

❶ Place fish in grilling basket. Spread both sides of each fillet liberally with mayonnaise and season with Old Bay seasoning. Lay 3 slices of bacon over mayonnaise on one side of fillet. Place at least two feet above flames of a campfire or over low heat (or low coals) on a grill, bacon side up. Cook approximately 20 minutes before turning bacon-side down, being careful not to burn mayonnaise. Cook an additional 20 minutes or until bacon begins to crisp and fish flakes easily with a fork.

2 servings.

EASY CAJUN GRILLED CATFISH

Jeff Havir
Phoenix, Arizona

1 large bottle Cajun-flavored marinade

6 (8 to 10 oz. each) catfish fillets

1/4 cup canola, olive or vegetable oil

❶ In large resealable plastic bag, combine marinade and fillets. Seal bag and refrigerate 6 to 8 hours. Remove fish from marinade; discard marinade.

❷ Heat grill on high and brush clean. Oil grill grates. Place fillets on grill; cook about 4 minutes on each side or until fish flakes easily with a fork.

6 servings.

SEA BASS SUPER BAKE

Carol Ann Sanderson
Bomey Lake, Washington

1 (5-lb.) sea bass, cleaned, head attached

1 sweet onion, thinly sliced

1 red bell pepper, seeded and sliced

2 lemons, thinly sliced

1/4 lb. asparagus, cleaned, uncut

1/4 cup extra-virgin olive oil

Fennel to taste

Rosemary to taste

Thyme to taste

❶ Heat grill.

❷ Place fish, with belly opening toward you, on large piece of aluminum foil (about 2½ times as long as the fish). Alternately layer fish with onion, bell pepper, lemons and asparagus. Sprinkle with olive oil, fennel, rosemary and thyme. Enclose fish in foil; poke holes into foil to allow steam to escape.

❸ Place on prepared grill and cook 15 minutes over hot coals. Turn packet over and grill an additional 15 minutes or until fish flakes easily with a fork.

8 servings.

GRILLED RAINBOW TROUT

Scott Wilson Sr.
West Unity, Ohio

6 rainbow trout, walleye or bass fillets, skin on

Juice of 1 large lemon

Garlic pepper to taste

6 tablespoons butter, cut into 12 pieces

1 onion, if desired, thinly sliced

6 tablespoons water

❶ Heat grill.

❷ Spray 3 large pieces of aluminum foil with cooking spray. Place two fillets, skin-side down, on each piece of foil; drizzle with lemon juice. Season with garlic pepper. Place two pieces of butter on each fillet; top with onion slices. Add 2 tablespoons water to each packet. Close packet and cook over medium coals 15 to 25 minutes or until fish flakes easily with a fork. Carefully remove fish from packet, remove skin, and serve with your favorite condiments.

6 servings.

GRILLED BASS

Michael Williams
Lemont Furnace, Pennsylvania

1/4 cup olive oil

Juice of 1 lime

Juice of 1 lemon

2 garlic cloves, chopped

1 tablespoon chopped fresh basil

Salt to taste

Freshly ground pepper to taste

2 lbs. bass

❶ In shallow dish, combine olive oil, lime juice, lemon juice, garlic, basil, salt and pepper; mix to blend. Add fish; coat well. Refrigerate 4 hours.

❷ Heat grill. Remove fish from marinade; discard marinade. Cook fish 4 to 8 minutes per side, turning once, or until fish flakes easily with a fork.

4 servings.

BBQ WALLEYE

Gerald Kuehn
Wautoma, Wisconsin

2 tablespoons soy sauce

2 tablespoons teriyaki sauce

1 tablespoon honey

1 tablespoon Cajun spice

1/2 teaspoon Worcestershire sauce

Salt to taste

Freshly ground pepper to taste

2 lbs. walleye fillets, cut into 1-inch-thick pieces

1 red bell pepper, cut into 1-inch-thick pieces

1 green bell pepper, cut into 1-inch-thick pieces

1 yellow bell pepper, cut into 1-inch-thick pieces

12 small whole onions, cut in half

❶ In large bowl, mix soy sauce, teriyaki sauce, honey, Cajun spice, Worcestershire sauce, salt and pepper. Coat walleye, peppers and onions in soy sauce mixture. Cover and refrigerate overnight.

❷ Heat grill. Remove fish and vegetables from marinade; discard marinade. Place fish, bell peppers and onions on 12-inch skewers. Grill over medium-high heat 4 to 6 minutes or until fish flakes easily with a fork.

4 servings.

CAJUN CAMPFIRE TROUT

H. C. "Papa" Meaux
Rolla, Missouri

1 tablespoon Cajun seasoning

2 (about 8 oz. each) trout

6 garlic cloves

2 teaspoons butter or margarine

2 bouquets garni of thyme, bay leaf and other herbs as desired

1 small onion, cut into 6 wedges

❶ Rub Cajun seasoning in cavity of trout. Make 3 diagonal slits in body of fish; stuff with garlic, butter, bouquets garni and onion wedges.

❷ Build medium-heat campfire. Cut 2 (18- x 14-inch) sheets of heavy-duty aluminum foil. Place 1 trout in center of each sheet. Fold long sides of foil together in locked folds. Fold and crimp short ends. Place packets directly on coals. Cook 4 minutes, then turn and cook an additional 4 to 6 minutes or until fish flakes easily with a fork.

❸ Remove bouquets garni and onion wedges; discard. Peel skin off trout and serve. Trout can be cooked in a barbecue pit or baked in a 350°F oven 15 to 20 minutes.

2 servings.

TROPICAL STYLE SNAPPER

John Sikking
Lakeland, Florida

¾ cup orange juice

¼ cup grapefruit juice

2 tablespoons fresh grated coconut

2 tablespoons honey

2 tablespoons fresh grated garlic

1 tablespoon soy sauce

2 (8-oz.) snapper, mahimahi, grouper, bass or
    speckled perch fillets, skin removed and deboned

Cayenne pepper to taste

¼ cup chopped fresh chives

¼ cup chopped fresh parsley

❶ In large glass baking dish, combine orange juice, grapefruit juice, coconut, honey, garlic and soy sauce; mix well. Add fillets and coat well. Refrigerate 30 minutes. Remove fillets from marinade; discard marinade.

❷ Heat grill. Sprinkle fillets with cayenne pepper, chives and parsley. Grill over medium heat until fish flakes easily with a fork, basting often. Remove from heat and serve hot. Serve with a cold citrus salad and sangria, if desired.

2 servings.

GLAZED GRILLED SALMON

Rick Dietz
Kingwood, Texas

1 tablespoon packed brown sugar

1 teaspoon honey

2 tablespoons unsalted butter

2 tablespoons Dijon mustard

3 tablespoons soy sauce

3 tablespoons teriyaki sauce

3 tablespoons orange juice

1 tablespoon olive oil

1 (2- to 2½-lb.) salmon fillet, skin on, about
    ¾ to 1 inch thick

❶ In small sauté pan, melt brown sugar, honey and butter over medium heat. Remove from heat and whisk in mustard, soy sauce, teriyaki sauce, orange juice and olive oil. Allow to cool. Place salmon, skin-side down, on large sheet of aluminum foil. Trim foil to leave ¼ to ½ inch around the edge of the salmon. Spread brown sugar mixture evenly over salmon.

❷ Heat grill. Grill salmon indirectly over medium heat until edges begin to brown and the inside is opaque, about 30 to 35 minutes. (With the lid of the grill closed, you do not need to flip the fish. The internal temperature should be around 125°F, and the sweet-and-sour glaze should have caramelized.) Turn off heat and, using large baking sheet, carefully transfer salmon with foil to cutting board. Cut salmon crosswise between the skin and flesh and remove salmon pieces to serving platter.

6 to 8 servings.

GLAZED GRILLED SALMON

Panfried,
Cakes, Patties
& Fillets

ASIAN FISH STIR-FRY

ASIAN FISH STIR-FRY

Gerald Kuehn
Wautoma, Wisconsin

¼ cup vegetable oil
2 lbs. fish fillets, cut into 1-inch pieces
1 cup sliced celery
1 cup sliced onions
1 cup sliced mushrooms
1 cup snow peas
1 garlic clove, minced
1 cup water
1 tablespoon cornstarch
1½ tablespoons soy sauce
¼ teaspoon ground ginger
½ teaspoon salt
2 tablespoons sherry

❶ In medium skillet, heat 3 tablespoons of the oil over medium-high heat until hot. Add fish; reduce heat to low and cook fish until firm. Remove fish from skillet. Add remaining oil to skillet. Add celery, onions, mushrooms, snow peas and garlic; cook and stir until vegetables are softened.

❷ In medium bowl, combine water, cornstarch, soy sauce, ginger, salt and sherry; blend well. Stir mixture in with vegetables. Add fish; cook until sauce is clear and fish flakes easily with a fork. Serve with rice, if desired.

6 servings.

BLACKENED WALLEYE

Wayne Smith
Thunder Bay, Ontario, Canada

4 tablespoons paprika
3 teaspoons chili powder
2 teaspoons onion powder
1 teaspoon dried oregano leaves
1 teaspoon garlic powder
1 teaspoon white pepper
1 teaspoon freshly ground black pepper
1 teaspoon cayenne pepper
1 teaspoon salt
4 (6 to 8 oz. each) skinless walleye fillets
1 stick butter or margarine

❶ In shallow bowl, combine paprika, chili powder, onion powder, oregano leaves, garlic powder, white pepper, black pepper, cayenne pepper and salt.

❷ Heat large, cast-iron skillet over a propane burner until pan becomes extremely hot (begins to turn white). It is best to do this outdoors for safety because of the extreme heat needed and the smoke that is created from burning the spice ingredients.

❸ Rinse walleye fillets and pat dry. In large saucepan, melt one half of the butter over medium heat. Coat both sides of fillets with butter, then dredge fillets in spice mixture until each side is evenly coated. Place fillets in heated cast-iron skillet and drizzle with remaining butter.

❹ Cook fillets about 6 minutes or until fish flakes easily with a fork, turning fillets every 60 seconds.

4 servings.

STU'S CRABBY PATTY

Stewart R. Barry
Hawaii National Park, Hawaii

½ lb. fresh crabmeat

¼ cup finely chopped green bell pepper

1 egg, slightly beaten

3 tablespoons mayonnaise

½ teaspoon paprika

¼ teaspoon cumin

¼ teaspoon ground ginger

¼ teaspoon cayenne pepper

¼ teaspoon onion powder

1 cup seasoned bread crumbs

⅔ cup oil

Buns

Tartar sauce

Sweet onions

Lettuce

❶ Pick through the crabmeat and discard any shell and cartilage.

❷ In large bowl, combine crabmeat, pepper, egg, mayonnaise, spices and bread crumbs; mix together until combined thoroughly. Form mixture into 4 patties.

❸ In large skillet, heat oil over medium-high heat until hot. Add patties; cook until golden brown. Serve on buns with tartar sauce, sweet onions and lettuce.

4 servings.

CAJUN RED SNAPPER

Richard Hansen
Burlington, Ontario, Canada

1 teaspoon paprika

¼ teaspoon cayenne pepper

1 teaspoon freshly ground pepper

½ teaspoon onion powder

1 teaspoon dried thyme

1 teaspoon dried basil

1 teaspoon garlic powder

¼ teaspoon dried oregano

2 tablespoons butter or margarine

1 tablespoon olive oil

6 (6-oz.) red snapper fillets

Salt to taste

❶ On large piece of parchment paper, mix together paprika, cayenne pepper, black pepper, onion powder, thyme, basil, garlic powder and oregano.

❷ In small saucepan, melt butter with oil over medium heat. Brush both sides of fillets with butter mixture; reserve remaining butter mixture. Coat both sides of fillets with seasoning mixture.

❸ Heat large cast-iron skillet over high heat until a drop of water sizzles on it. Drizzle half of the remaining butter-oil mixture on one side of fish fillets. Place fillets butter-side down in skillet. Cook over high heat until fish is deeply browned, about 5 minutes. Drizzle remaining butter mixture over fish, then turn fish over. Cook until fish is browned and flakes easily with a fork, about an additional 5 minutes. Season with salt.

6 servings.

BLACKENED CATFISH

Chris Belote
Altamonte Springs, Florida

1 teaspoon paprika

$1/2$ teaspoon dried oregano, crumbled

$1/2$ teaspoon dried thyme, crumbled

$1/4$ teaspoon cayenne pepper

$1/2$ teaspoon sugar

$1/2$ teaspoon salt

$1/2$ teaspoon freshly ground pepper

2 (8-oz.) catfish fillets

1 tablespoon olive oil

1 garlic clove, sliced thin

1 tablespoon butter

Lemon wedges

❶ In small bowl, combine paprika, oregano, thyme, cayenne pepper, sugar, salt and freshly ground pepper. Rinse catfish and pat dry. Rub both sides of fillets with spices.

❷ In large skillet, heat oil over medium-high heat until hot. Add garlic; sauté, stirring often, until golden brown. Remove garlic from skillet and add butter; heat until foam subsides. Add fillets to saucepan; sauté 4 minutes on each side or until fish flakes easily with a fork. Serve with lemon wedges.

2 servings.

SOUTHERN FRIED FLUKE FILLET

Leslie Richardson
San Benito, Texas

$1/2$ cup all-purpose flour

$1/2$ teaspoon salt

$1/4$ teaspoon freshly ground pepper

$1 1/2$ cups finely chopped pecans

$1 1/2$ cups soft bread crumbs

4 (8-oz.) fish fillets

2 large eggs, beaten

3 tablespoons butter or margarine, melted

3 tablespoons vegetable oil

❶ In shallow dish, combine flour, salt and pepper; stir well and set aside. In another shallow dish, combine pecans and bread crumbs; stir well and set aside. Dredge fillets in flour mixture, dip in beaten egg, then coat with pecan mixture.

❷ In large skillet, heat butter and oil over medium heat until hot. Add fillets; cook 3 to 4 minutes on each side or until fish flakes easily with a fork. Drain well.

4 servings.

TUNA PATTIES

Pat Girsh
Broaddus, Texas

1 (16-oz.) can albacore tuna, drained

1 egg, slightly beaten

$1/3$ cup water

$1/3$ cup cornmeal

Vegetable oil

❶ In medium bowl, combine tuna, egg, water and cornmeal. Form tuna mixture into 4 patties.

❷ In large skillet, heat oil over medium-high heat until hot. Add tuna patties; cook 5 to 6 minutes or until golden brown on both sides. Serve with macaroni and cheese and fresh vegetable of choice, if desired.

2 to 4 servings.

WALLEYE ROLL-UPS

Joyce Gordon
Stettler, Alberta, Canada

4 tablespoons butter, divided
1 small onion, chopped
6 fresh mushrooms
4 (6 to 8 oz. each) walleye fillets, cut into 2-inch strips
4 oz. cream cheese, softened
2 eggs, scrambled in bowl (egg wash)
1 cup seasoned bread crumbs (seasonings: 1/2 teaspoon salt, 1/4 teaspoon freshly ground pepper, 1/4 teaspoon garlic salt and 1/4 teaspoon paprika)

❶ In large skillet, melt 2 tablespoons of the butter over medium heat. Add onions and mushrooms; sauté 3 to 5 minutes or until soft. Meanwhile, pound fillets to 1/4-inch thickness.

❷ In large bowl, mix together onions, mushrooms and cream cheese. Spread mixture evenly onto fillets. Roll up fillets; secure with toothpicks. Coat roll-ups with egg wash, then roll in seasoned bread crumbs.

❸ Add fillets to skillet; fry 6 to 8 minutes or until golden brown on each side and fish flakes easily with a fork. Serve with your favorite coleslaw and choice of potatoes.

4 servings.

SALMON CAKES

Jim Netzel
Chicago, Illinois

4 cups water
1 cup dry white wine
4 celery sprigs
6 parsley sprigs
6 whole peppercorns
1 teaspoon salt
1 (1-lb.) salmon fillet
1 1/4 cups bread crumbs (divided)
1 tablespoon chopped fresh thyme or 1 teaspoon dry
1 teaspoon dried oregano
1/2 teaspoon dry mustard
Dash of cayenne pepper
Salt to taste
Freshly ground pepper to taste
1 cup light mayonnaise
1/2 cup diced onion
1/2 cup diced celery
1 tablespoon chopped capers
1 tablespoon chopped fresh parsley
1 large egg, beaten
2 tablespoons canola oil

❶ In large pot, bring water, white wine, celery, parsley, peppercorns and salt to a boil, then reduce to a simmer. Add salmon; cook 10 minutes or until salmon flakes easily with a fork. Remove salmon and let cool; flake into large bowl.

❷ In another large bowl, combine 1/4 cup of the bread crumbs, thyme, oregano, mustard, cayenne, salt and pepper. Add flaked salmon, mayonnaise, onion, celery, capers, parsley and egg. Place remaining bread crumbs in shallow dish. Gently form salmon mixture into 8 (2 1/2-inch) patties about 3/4 inch thick. Coat patties in remaining bread crumbs. Cover and refrigerate 1 hour.

❸ In large skillet, heat oil over medium heat until hot. Add salmon patties; sauté 4 to 6 minutes, turning once, until golden brown.

4 servings.

ASIAN PANFRIED WALLEYE CAKES

Nam Nguyen
Burnsville, Minnesota

1 red bell pepper, diced

3 tablespoons vegetable oil

1 lb. baked walleye, chilled, boneless and skinless, cut into chunks

1 tablespoon finely chopped fresh garlic

1 to 2 jalapeño peppers, seeded and finely chopped

1/4 cup mayonnaise

2 tablespoons Old Bay seasoning

6 slices fresh white bread, crusts removed, processed into fine crumbs

Salt to taste

Freshly ground pepper to taste

Tabasco sauce

❶ In small pan, sauté diced red bell pepper in 1 tablespoon of the oil until softened, about 2 to 4 minutes.

❷ In medium bowl, combine walleye, sautéed red bell pepper, garlic, jalapeño peppers and mayonnaise. Add seasoning powder, 2 tablespoons of the bread crumbs, salt and pepper. Form 8 equal-sized patties approximately 1/4 inch thick. Coat each cake with bread crumbs. Refrigerate at least 1 hour.

❸ In medium skillet, heat remaining 2 tablespoons oil over medium heat until hot. Add cakes; sauté until golden brown, turning once, 4 to 6 minutes. Serve with Tabasco sauce.

4 servings.

SIMPLE FISH FILLET

Leslie Richardson
San Benito, Texas

2 lbs. fish fillets

1/4 cup all-purpose flour

1 teaspoon salt

Freshly ground pepper

1 teaspoon paprika

2 tablespoons olive oil

1/2 cup blanched slivered almonds

3 tablespoons lemon juice

1 tablespoon chopped fresh parsley

Lemon wedges

❶ Wash and dry fillets. On parchment paper, mix flour, salt, pepper and paprika. Dredge fillets lightly in seasoned flour.

❷ In large, heavy skillet, heat oil over medium heat until hot. Add fillets; fry about 6 to 8 minutes on both sides or until lightly browned and fish flakes easily with a fork. Remove fish to ovenproof platter and keep warm. Add almonds to skillet and lightly brown. Sprinkle almonds with lemon juice and pour pan juices and almonds over fillets. Garnish with parsley and lemon wedges.

4 servings.

CRAPPIE CROQUETTES

Bradley Stringfield
Oliver Springs, Tennessee

2 cups cooked flaked crappie

1 cup bread crumbs

1 tablespoon parsley

Dash of freshly ground pepper

Dash of paprika

1 tablespoon lemon juice

4 tablespoons butter

½ teaspoon salt

4 tablespoons all-purpose flour

1 cup plus 4 tablespoons milk

2 eggs

1 cup cracker crumbs

¼ cup canola oil

❶ In large bowl, combine flaked crappie, bread crumbs, parsley, pepper and paprika; mix until well blended. Set aside.

❷ In large saucepan, melt butter over medium heat. Add salt and flour. Whisk in 1 cup of the milk and reduce heat to low. Cook until mixture thickens; set aside to cool.

❸ Add crappie mixture to butter mixture; refrigerate 30 minutes. Meanwhile, beat eggs with remaining 4 tablespoons milk. Remove crappie mixture from refrigerator and form croquettes or balls with hands, then dip in egg mixture. Roll croquettes in cracker crumbs, then dip again in egg mixture. Roll once more in cracker crumbs.

❹ In large, deep skillet, heat oil over medium heat until hot. Add croquettes; cook 4 to 6 minutes or until brown. Drain on paper towels.

4 servings.

BY THE BROOK TROUT A LA DONNY

Donny Tindall
Muncie, Indiana

2 teaspoons lemon peel

¼ cup chopped fresh basil

1 teaspoon Worcestershire sauce

¼ cup extra-virgin olive oil

½ cup chopped macadamia nuts

8 brook trout

8 thin, wide slices Canadian bacon

2 tablespoons butter

❶ In small bowl, combine lemon peel, basil and Worcestershire sauce. In small sauté pan, heat oil over high heat until hot. Add lemon peel mixture; sauté 1½ minutes until scorched. Remove pan from heat and stir in nuts. Divide mixture between trout and place in cavity. Wrap in Canadian bacon; secure with string.

❷ In large skillet, melt butter over medium-high heat. Add fish; cook 3 minutes per side or until fish flakes easily with a fork. Serve on a platter of polenta and garnish with rosemary sprigs. Serve with Riesling, if desired.

8 servings.

KAUAI'S BROILED SALMON PATTIES WITH SPICY CHILI SAUCE

Earl Okuda
Salt Lake City, Utah

1 (1-lb.) salmon fillet

2 tablespoons sesame oil

1 tablespoon sesame seeds

2 green onions, finely chopped

Sriracha hot chili sauce

¼ cup mayonnaise

❶ Break salmon into ¼-inch chunks and place in large bowl. Add 1 tablespoon of the sesame oil, sesame seeds and 1 chopped green onion; mix well. Form 4 equal-sized patties. Place patties on aluminum foil. Broil about 2 minutes or until top is brown and fish flakes easily with a fork. Remove patties from broiler and drizzle with chili sauce.

❷ In small bowl, combine mayonnaise, 2 tablespoons of the chili sauce and remaining tablespoon sesame oil; mix well. Serve alongside patties. Garnish with remaining green onion.

4 servings.

SNOOK BURGERS

John Sikking
Lakeland, Florida

1 lb. shaved snook (or crab meat)

2½ cups Italian bread crumbs

1 egg, beaten

¾ cup mayonnaise or salad dressing

⅓ cup chopped celery

⅓ cup chopped green bell pepper

⅓ cup chopped onion

1 tablespoon Old Bay seasoning

1 tablespoon minced fresh parsley

2 tablespoons fresh lemon juice

1 teaspoon Worcestershire sauce

1 teaspoon prepared mustard

¼ teaspoon freshly ground pepper

¼ teaspoon Tabasco sauce

2 to 4 tablespoons olive oil

❶ In large bowl, combine snook, bread crumbs, egg, mayonnaise, celery, green pepper, onion, Old Bay seasoning, parsley, lemon juice, Worcestershire sauce, mustard, pepper and Tabasco; mix well. Form mixture into 8 patties.

❷ In large skillet, heat oil over medium-high heat until hot. Add patties; sauté 4 to 6 minutes or until golden brown. Serve on buns with lemon slices on the side.

8 servings.

NORTHEAST SHORE FISH CAKES

Leslie Richardson
San Benito, Texas

6 tablespoons butter or margarine, divided

1/3 cup chopped green onions

2 cups mashed potatoes

1 tablespoon sour cream

1 lb. cod, cooked and flaked

1 large egg, beaten

2 to 3 tablespoons minced fresh parsley

1/2 teaspoon dry mustard

1/4 teaspoon salt

1/8 teaspoon freshly ground pepper

1/2 to 3/4 cup Italian seasoned bread crumbs

1 tablespoons olive oil

❶ In large skillet, melt 2 tablespoons of the butter over medium heat. Add green onions; sauté until tender and set aside.

❷ In medium bowl, combine mashed potatoes, 2 tablespoons of the butter and sour cream; mix well. Gently stir in fish. Set aside.

❸ In another medium bowl, combine egg, parsley, mustard, salt and pepper. Stir in reserved green onions. Add green onion mixture to fish mixture, stirring gently. Shape fish mixture into 8 patties, then dredge in bread crumbs.

❹ Melt remaining 2 tablespoons butter over medium heat in large skillet. Add patties; cook 3 minutes on each side or until lightly browned.

4 servings.

SALMON BURGERS

William Biacco
Oakdale, Pennsylvania

3 tablespoons butter or margarine, divided

1/2 cup chopped onion

1 (14.75-oz.) can or 2 cups cooked salmon

2 eggs, slightly beaten

1/2 cup Italian bread crumbs or cracker crumbs

1 tablespoon lemon juice

Salt to taste

Freshly ground pepper to taste

3 drops Tabasco sauce

❶ In medium saucepan, melt 1 tablespoon of the butter over medium heat. Add onion; sauté 2 to 4 minutes or until onion is soft. Flake salmon and mix with sautéed onions, eggs, bread crumbs, lemon juice, salt, pepper and Tabasco. Form mixture into 4 patties.

❷ In large skillet, sauté patties in remaining 2 tablespoons butter over medium heat until browned on both sides, about 4 to 6 minutes. Serve on hamburger buns with favorite toppings.

4 servings.

PANKO PARMESAN WALLEYE

Edward Janas
Pleasanton, California

1 egg

1/2 cup milk

1 cup Panko (Japanese) bread crumbs

1/2 cup shredded Parmesan cheese

4 (6- to 8-oz.) walleye fillets

2 tablespoons olive oil

❶ Heat oven to 375°F.

❷ In medium bowl, mix egg and milk together; beat lightly.

❸ In another medium bowl, mix together bread crumbs and Parmesan cheese. Dip fillets in the egg mixture, then coat with bread-crumb mixture.

❹ In large, ovenproof skillet, heat oil over medium-high heat until hot. Add fillets; sear both sides. Remove fish to oven and bake 10 to 15 minutes or until fish flakes easily with a fork.

4 servings.

SALMON BURGERS

Crusts, Rubs
& Marinades

GRILLED MARINATED BASS FILLETS

Michael Williams
Lemont Furnace, Pennsylvania

¼ cup olive oil
Juice of 1 lime
Juice of 1 lemon
2 garlic cloves, chopped
1 tablespoon chopped fresh basil
½ teaspoon salt
¼ teaspoon freshly ground pepper
2 lbs. bass fillets

❶ In shallow dish, combine olive oil, juices of lime and lemon, garlic, basil, salt and pepper; mix to blend. Add fish and coat well. Cover and refrigerate at least 4 hours. Remove fish from marinade; discard marinade.

❷ Heat grill. Cook fish over medium-high heat 4 to 8 minutes per side, turning only once, until fish flakes easily with a fork.

4 servings.

WINE MARINATED SALMON

San Wichner
San Pablo, California

½ cup rosé wine
¼ cup light soy sauce
⅛ cup lemon juice
3 garlic cloves, minced
2 scallions, diced
½ medium onion, diced
1 tablespoon Dijon mustard
⅛ teaspoon Tabasco sauce, if desired
1 (2-lb). salmon fillet, skinned
3 tablespoons butter

❶ In large, resealable plastic bag, combine wine, soy sauce, lemon juice, garlic, scallions, onion, Dijon mustard and Tabasco; mix well. Add fish; refrigerate at least 2 hours. Remove fish and marinade to large skillet; bring to a boil, then cover and simmer 15 minutes or until fish flakes easily with a fork. Remove fish. Add butter to skillet and bring to a boil, then simmer until sauce thickens. Serve fish over herbal rice and pour sauce over all.

4 servings.

ONION-DIJON CRUSTED CATFISH

Andrew J. Krotje
Brooksville, Florida

1 onion, finely chopped
¼ cup honey Dijon mustard
4 (6-oz.) catfish fillets
Garlic salt to taste
Freshly ground pepper to taste
1 tablespoon chopped fresh parsley

❶ Heat oven to 350°F.

❷ In small bowl, mix onion and mustard. Season fillets with garlic salt and pepper. Place fillets on baking sheet; coat evenly with onion mixture. Sprinkle parsley evenly over fillets. Bake 20 minutes or until fish flakes easily with a fork. Turn oven to broil and broil until golden, about 3 to 5 minutes.

4 servings.

HONEY LEMON GRILLED CATFISH

Joseph Vuono
Hanover, Pennsylvania

1/2 cup honey

2 tablespoons lemon juice

1 lb. catfish fillets

Old Bay seasoning, to taste

1 lemon, sliced

❶ In small bowl, mix honey and lemon juice. Brush each side of fillet evenly with honey mixture. Place fish on aluminum foil and sprinkle with Old Bay seasoning.

❷ Heat grill. Cook fish over medium heat until fish flakes easily with a fork, about 6 to 8 minutes, continually basting with honey mixture. Just before serving, season again with Old Bay. Garnish with lemon slices.

2 to 4 servings.

MARINATED SALMON

Ed Janas
Pleasanton, California

1 cup olive oil

2 to 3 cups soy sauce

2 cups packed brown sugar

Kosher (coarse) salt to taste

Freshly ground pepper to taste

Dry mustard to taste

3 to 4 garlic cloves, chopped

2 cans (6-oz.) orange juice concentrate

4 (8-oz.) center-cut salmon fillets, skin on

❶ In large bowl, combine olive oil, soy sauce, brown sugar, salt, pepper, dry mustard, garlic and orange juice; mix well. Stir in salmon; cover and refrigerate 3 hours or overnight. Remove salmon from marinade; discard marinade.

❷ Heat grill. Cook salmon, skin-side down, 6 to 10 minutes or until fish flakes easily with a fork. Skin will blacken and stick to grill. With spatula, remove salmon leaving skin on grill. Serve hot with favorite veggies and lemon-honey rice (add grated lemon peel and honey to cooked white rice).

4 servings.

CAROL'S SALMON SALSA WITH BUTTER

Tony Fabrizio
Burbank, California

1/2 cup tomato salsa (mild or hot)

1/4 cup lime juice

1/4 cup butter, melted

1 tablespoon olive oil

1 teaspoon Dijon mustard

1/2 garlic clove, minced

Salt to taste

Freshly ground pepper to taste

4 (6-oz.) salmon fillets

❶ In food processor, puree salsa, lime juice, butter, olive oil, mustard, garlic, salt and pepper. Place salmon fillets in 13x9-inch glass baking dish and cover both sides with puree. Refrigerate 1 hour.

❷ Heat oven to 375°F. Cover fillets with aluminum foil and bake 35 to 45 minutes or until fish flakes easily with a fork.

4 servings.

HONEY LEMON GRILLED CATFISH

SALMON WITH DILL RUB

SALMON WITH DILL RUB

Allen Kelly
APO AE 90123

DILL RUB

4 tablespoons dill

2 teaspoons coarse salt

1 teaspoon freshly ground pepper

FISH

4 (1-inch-thick) salmon steaks

CUCUMBER AND DILL RELISH

1 English cucumber, peeled and diced

1 small onion, minced

1/4 cup sugar, or to taste

1/2 teaspoon kosher (coarse) salt, or to taste

12 tablespoons white vinegar

1/4 teaspoon freshly ground pepper, or to taste

❶ Prepare Rub: In small bowl, combine dill, salt and pepper. Coat salmon evenly with rub.

❷ Prepare Relish: In medium bowl, stir together cucumber, onion, sugar, salt, vinegar and pepper.

❸ Heat grill; oil grill grate and fish. Grill salmon medium high about 5 minutes per side or until firm in the center. Serve topped with relish.

4 servings.

CAROL'S FISH CHOWDER FOR FOUR

Tony Fabrizio
Burbank, California

1 1/4 lbs. cod, bass, or sheephead fillets

2 tablespoons unsalted butter

1 small onion, sliced

1/2 cup diced celery

2 garlic cloves, finely diced

2 cups boiling water

2 cups raw potatoes, diced

1/2 cup sliced carrots

1 teaspoon salt

1 teaspoon freshly ground pepper

1 cup half-and-half

3 tablespoons all-purpose flour

❶ Cut fillets into 1 1/2-inch-square pieces. In large saucepan, melt butter over medium-high heat. Add onion, celery and garlic; cook until onion is soft and transparent. Add boiling water, potatoes, carrots, salt and pepper; cover and simmer 10 to 15 minutes or until vegetables are soft. Add fish; cook 10 minutes more until fish flakes easily with a fork. Stir in half-and-half and flour; reheat but do not boil.

4 servings.

BAKED SALMON II

Andrew J. Krotje
Brooksville, Florida

2 garlic cloves, minced

6 tablespoons light olive oil

1 teaspoon dried basil

1 teaspoon salt

1 teaspoon freshly ground pepper

1 tablespoon lemon juice

1 tablespoon chopped fresh parsley

2 (6-oz.) salmon fillets

❶ In medium bowl, combine garlic, olive oil, basil, salt, pepper, lemon juice and parsley; mix well. Place salmon fillets in medium glass baking dish; cover with the marinade. Refrigerate 1 hour, turning occasionally.

❷ Heat oven to 375°F. Place fillets in aluminum foil, cover with marinade and seal. Place sealed salmon in baking dish and cook 35 to 45 minutes or until fish flakes easily with a fork.

2 servings.

BOURBON GRILLED SALMON

Michael McClure
Dewitt, Michigan

¼ cup pineapple juice

2 tablespoons soy sauce

2 tablespoons packed brown sugar

1 teaspoon bourbon

¼ teaspoon freshly ground pepper

⅛ teaspoon garlic powder

½ cup vegetable oil

2 (8-oz.) salmon fillets

❶ In large bowl, combine juice, soy sauce, brown sugar, bourbon, pepper, garlic powder and oil; mix well. Remove all skin, fat and dark meat from salmon. Pour ¾ of the marinade over salmon in glass dish or large, resealable plastic bag; reserve remaining ¼ marinade. Refrigerate at least 1 hour.

❷ Heat grill. Remove fillets from marinade and cook over medium heat 5 to 10 minutes or until fish flakes easily with a fork. Baste with reserved marinade.

2 servings.

Soups, Salads
& Sandwiches

SMOKED SALMON SCRAMBLE

John Anderson
Anderson, California

¼ cup butter

8 eggs, lightly beaten

4 tablespoons heavy cream

8 oz. skinless boneless smoked salmon or trout, flaked

2 tablespoons chopped fresh mixed herbs (such as chives, basil and parsley)

4 English muffins, split

Extra butter for spreading

Chopped fresh chives

Salt to taste

Freshly ground pepper to taste

Lemon wedges

❶ In large skillet, melt butter over medium heat. When it begins to foam, add eggs. Slowly stir and move eggs around in pan to allow even cooking. Before eggs set, stir in heavy cream, flaked salmon and chopped herbs. Stir to incorporate. Do not overcook eggs.

❷ Meanwhile, toast muffins. Spread with butter and place 2 muffin halves on each of 4 serving plates. When eggs are done, divide evenly between the muffins. Sprinkle with a few chopped chives, season to taste, and serve warm with a lemon wedge.

4 servings.

MOM'S BEST CRAPPIE SANDWICH

Larry Pacewicz
San Leandro, California

4 (8 to 10 oz. each) crappie fillets

2 cups whole milk

½ cup white cornmeal

½ cup cornstarch

½ cup all-purpose flour

2 tablespoons chili powder

1 tablespoon salt

2 cups canola oil

8 slices rye bread (or other bread of choice)

Tabasco or tartar sauce

❶ In large container, soak crappie fillets in whole milk 1 hour. In large, resealable plastic bag, combine cornmeal, cornstarch, flour, chili powder and salt. Remove fillets from milk; discard milk. Add fillets to resealable plastic bag; shake fillets with dry ingredients.

❷ In large skillet, heat oil over medium-high heat until hot. Place fillets in skillet; fry until golden brown, about 3 to 5 minutes. Place fillets on bread and serve with Tabasco or tartar sauce.

4 servings.

MOM'S BEST CRAPPIE SANDWICH

ELI'S FISH TACOS

Eli Stancliff
Crescent City, California

1 lb. fish fillets

2 limes

Salsa

Corn tortillas (fried into a taco shell shape) or
hard taco shells

Chopped fresh cilantro

❶ Heat oven to 375°F. Place fish in baking pan.
Squeeze the juice of 1 lime over the fish and top with
1 tablespoon salsa. Bake 10 to 15 minutes or until
fish flakes easily with a fork. Spoon fish and pan
juices into taco shells; sprinkle with cilantro. Serve
with a squeeze of lime juice and salsa.

4 servings.

SALMON ROLLS

Steve Brown
Klawock, Alaska

1 loaf frozen bread dough, thawed

1 (3-oz.) pkg. cream cheese, softened

1 lb. cooked, flaked salmon

2 cups spinach leaves

1/2 cup (2 oz.) grated cheddar cheese

Dijon mustard

❶ Heat oven to 375°F. Spray baking sheet with
nonstick cooking spray.

❷ Let bread dough rise until doubled; punch
down and roll out to 8x14-inch rectangle.

❸ Spread cream cheese evenly over dough and
top with flaked salmon and single layer of spinach
leaves. Roll dough starting with the long edge;
pinch dough to seal. Cut dough into 1- to 2-inch-
thick rolls.

❹ Place rolls on prepared baking sheet; let rise
30 minutes. Sprinkle with grated Cheddar cheese
and bake 30 to 45 minutes or until golden brown.
Serve with Dijon mustard.

About 1 dozen rolls.

SALMON-PASTA SALAD

Gene and Dorothy Zamora
Benton City, Washington

SALMON

1 (1/2-lb.) salmon fillet or 1/2 lb. canned salmon

1/8 teaspoon dill weed

Salt to taste

Freshly ground pepper to taste

Granulated garlic to taste

2 tablespoons olive oil

PASTA

2 1/2 cups extra-wide noodles, cooked according to
package directions and drained

1 cup halved olives

1/4 cup finely chopped carrots

2 ribs celery, finely chopped

1/2 cup finely chopped tomato

1/4 cup finely chopped green onions

1/4 cup finely chopped red onion

SAUCE

5 tablespoons butter, melted

1/8 teaspoon dill weed

3/4 tablespoon granulated garlic

2 freshly squeezed lemons

Salt to taste

Freshly ground pepper to taste

❶ For Salmon: Sprinkle salmon with dill weed,
salt, pepper and granulated garlic. In large skillet,
heat oil over medium-high heat until hot. Add
salmon; cook 2 minutes per side or until fish flakes
easily with a fork.

❷ For Pasta: In large bowl, stir together noodles,
olives, carrots, celery, tomato, green onions and red
onion. Flake salmon and gently stir into noodle
mixture.

❸ For Sauce: In large, microwave-safe bowl, stir
together butter, dill weed, granulated garlic,
lemon juice, salt and pepper; cook in microwave on
high 1 1/2 minutes. Gently stir sauce into pasta. Serve
warm with toasted French bread.

4 servings.

SCAMPI SEAFOOD STEW

Steve Petroff
Beaumont, California

1/4 lb. shrimp, peeled and cut in half lengthwise
    (shells reserved)

1 cup unsalted chicken stock

1/4 cup dry vermouth

1/4 lb. squid, cut into 1/4-inch rings and tentacles
    cut in half

4 quaquog clams, removed from shell, cleaned, and
    liquor reserved

1/4 cup chopped fresh parsley

1 tablespoon chopped fresh basil

1 teaspoon fresh chopped thyme or oregano

2 garlic cloves, minced

2 tablespoons olive oil

2 tablespoons butter

1/3 cup sliced red onion

2 anchovy fillets, mashed

1/2 lemon, juiced

❶ Place shrimp shells, chicken stock and vermouth in medium saucepan. Simmer until reduced by half; strain and discard shells. Mix squid and clams with half of the chopped parsley, basil, thyme (or oregano) and garlic; refrigerate until ready to cook.

❷ In Dutch oven, heat olive oil and butter. Add red onions and sauté 3 to 5 minutes or until soft. Add anchovies and remaining herbs and garlic; sauté 1 to 2 minutes. Add chicken stock and juice from lemon; bring to a simmer. Add shrimp; cook 1 minute. Add seafood mixture; cook 1 to 2 minutes. Garnish with lemons and parsley.

4 to 6 servings.

CATFISH SOUP

William Cook
Dexter, Missouri

4 slices bacon, cut into 1/2-inch pieces

1 tablespoon olive oil

1 onion, finely chopped

2 ribs celery, finely chopped

2 carrots, finely chopped

3 garlic cloves, minced

1/2 cup all-purpose flour

1/2 teaspoon kosher (coarse) salt

1/4 teaspoon paprika

4 cups 1% milk

5 cups fat-free chicken broth

2 medium potatoes, cut into 1/2-inch pieces

1 1/2 to 2 lbs. catfish fillets, cut into 1 1/2-inch pieces

1/2 cup (2 oz.) shredded fat-free cheddar cheese

❶ In large Dutch oven, sauté bacon until crisp. Add olive oil, onion, celery, carrots and garlic; sauté until vegetables are softened. Stir in flour, salt and paprika. Whisk in milk and chicken broth. Add potatoes, stirring until soup thickens. Cook 10 minutes or until potatoes are tender. Stir in catfish and cheddar cheese; cook an additional 10 to 15 minutes.

8 servings.

GREEN BEAN SALAD WITH GRILLED FILLETS

GREEN BEAN SALAD WITH GRILLED FILLETS

Andrew J. Krotje
Brooksville, Florida

4 fillets, your choice

2 tablespoons melted butter

1 tablespoon fresh lemon juice

1 lb. fresh or frozen green beans, cooked, chilled in ice water

1/4 red onion, thinly sliced

4 oz. cherry tomatoes, cut in half

1/4 cup fresh basil, chopped

1/2 cup balsamic Italian salad dressing

❶ Heat grill.

❷ Brush fillets with melted butter. Squeeze fresh lemon juice over fillets.

❸ Grill fillets 5 to 7 minutes, turning once, until fish flakes easily with a fork. Toss beans, onion, cherry tomatoes, basil and dressing together. Top with grilled fillets.

4 servings.

CRAPPIE CHOWDER

Lynn Donovan
Middleville, Michigan

1/4 cup diced salt pork

1/3 cup chopped onion

1 1/2 cups diced potatoes

1 cup water

Salt to taste

Freshly ground pepper to taste

1/4 teaspoon thyme

1 1/2 lbs. boneless crappie fillets, diced into 1-inch pieces

1 can creamed corn

2 cups milk

❶ In large saucepan, sauté pork until almost crisp. Add onion; cook until tender. Add potatoes, water, salt, pepper, thyme and fish; cover and cook about 10 to 15 minutes or until fish flakes easily with fork. Gently stir in corn and milk; simmer until hot.

4 to 6 servings.

CHEEK MEAT APPETIZERS

Gerald Kuehn
Wautoma, Wisconsin

6 slices bacon, cut in half

Walleye or pike cheek meat (12 cheeks), or scallops

1/4 teaspoon garlic salt

2 tablespoons butter

1/4 cup peach marmalade

❶ In large skillet, fry bacon over medium heat until about halfway cooked. Wrap each cheek meat with 1/2 slice of bacon; secure with a toothpick. Sprinkle with garlic salt.

❷ In same skillet, melt butter over medium-high heat. Add fish; cook 3 to 5 minutes, turning once, until fish flakes easily with a fork and bacon is crispy. Before serving, top each cheek with 1 teaspoon peach marmalade.

4 servings.

CJ'S CRAPPIE SALAD

Jack Kimbro
Marion, Iowa

4 cups lettuce, torn

2 tomatoes, cut in wedges

1 cup sliced cucumber

¼ red onion, sliced

½ red bell pepper, sliced

4 (4 to 5 oz. each) crappie fillets

½ teaspoon salt

¼ teaspoon freshly ground pepper

3 tablespoons olive oil

½ cup ranch dressing

❶ In large bowl, toss lettuce, tomatoes, cucumbers, red onion and bell peppers. Season fillets with salt and pepper.

❷ In large saucepan, heat oil over medium-high heat until hot. Add fillets; sauté until browned and fish flakes easily with a fork, about 4 to 6 minutes.

Top salad with fish and serve with ranch dressing.

4 to 6 servings.

ELEGANT SEAFOOD CHOWDER

Ray Bebee
West Chicago, Illinois

½ lb. bacon, cut into ½-inch pieces

1 large onion, medium chopped

1 teaspoon dried thyme

1½ cups all-purpose flour

1 quart clam juice

2 lbs. red potatoes, medium diced and cooked

4 lbs. assorted fish and shellfish (clams, mussels, shelled shrimp, crabmeat, cod fillet)

1 pint milk

1 pint heavy cream

¼ teaspoon salt

¼ teaspoon freshly ground pepper

3 tablespoons butter

3 tablespoons chopped fresh parsley

❶ In large saucepan, sauté bacon over medium heat. Add onion and continue sautéing until onion is translucent. With whisk, stir in thyme and flour. Add clam juice and bring to a boil while whisking constantly. Add diced potatoes and fish. Add milk, cream, salt and pepper.

❷ Cover pan and simmer 15 to 20 minutes or until clams and mussels open and cod flakes easily with a fork. Serve in warm bowls with 1 teaspoon butter and sprinkles of fresh parsley.

8 servings.

FISH CHOWDER

Richard Hansen
Burlington, Ontario, Canada

3 ribs celery, diced

3 carrots, peeled and diced

2 large onions, diced

Water to cover vegetables

¼ cup butter

2 tablespoons all-purpose flour

4 cups milk or cream

4 potatoes, peeled and cubed

¼ teaspoon salt

¼ teaspoon freshly ground pepper

¼ teaspoon chopped fresh basil

1 garlic clove, minced

1½ lbs. lean fish fillets, cubed

½ lb. sharp cheddar cheese, grated

½ cup cooked and crumbled bacon

❶ In large saucepan, cover celery, carrots and onions with water; boil and cook 5 minutes. Reduce heat and simmer 3 minutes. Drain vegetables and set aside. Reserve water in pan and set aside.

❷ In small saucepan, melt butter over medium heat. Add flour; stir until creamy. Slowly whisk into vegetable water. Add cream and continue to whisk until mixture has thickened. Add vegetables and potatoes. Stir in salt, pepper, basil and garlic; simmer 45 minutes or until potatoes are tender, stirring frequently. Add fish; simmer 5 minutes. Ladle into bowls; top with cheese and bacon.

4 servings.

WALLEYE SOUP

Bob Cooper
Naples, New York

1½ lbs. walleye, perch or haddock fillets, skinless and cut into 1-inch pieces (skin reserved)

2 cups water

1 medium onion, finely chopped

3 tablespoons butter

2 medium potatoes, diced

1 cup whipping cream

1 cup half-and-half

Salt to taste

Freshly ground pepper to taste

❶ In large saucepan, cook fish and reserved skin in water; simmer and cook 5 minutes. Remove from heat and set aside.

❷ In large Dutch oven, sauté onion in butter 3 to 5 minutes or until softened. Add reserved fish liquid; discard skin. Add potatoes and cook about 10 minutes or until tender. Add cream, half-and-half and fish, then bring to a simmer. Season with salt and pepper.

4 servings.

HALIBUT FISH TACOS

Rick Dietz
Kingwood, Texas

2 lbs. halibut fillets

Extra-virgin olive oil

Salt to taste

Freshly ground pepper to taste

Juice of 1 lime

2 small avocados, pitted and scooped from skins

Juice of 1 lemon

1 teaspoon kosher (coarse) salt

½ teaspoon cayenne pepper

1 cup plain yogurt

2 plum tomatoes, seeded and diced

2 scallions, thinly sliced at an angle

12 (6-inch) flour tortillas

1 cup shredded purple cabbage

❶ Heat grill.

❷ Drizzle halibut with olive oil and season with salt and pepper. Grill fish over high heat 5 to 7 minutes on each side or until fish flakes easily with a fork. Squeeze lime juice over fish and remove from grill. Flake fish into large chunks with fork.

❸ While the fish is cooking, place avocado, lemon juice, coarse salt, cayenne pepper and yogurt in blender; mix until smooth. Place guacamole mixture in medium bowl and stir in tomatoes and scallions.

❹ Heat tortillas. To assemble the taco, place fish chunks into warm tortilla and smother with guacamole sauce. Top with shredded cabbage. Fold tacos and serve.

6 servings.

FISH GUMBO

Dan Barta
Elyria, Ohio

½ lb. bacon, diced

¼ cup all-purpose flour

8 cups chicken broth

1 cup diced onion

1 cup diced celery

1 cup diced red bell pepper

1 cup diced green bell pepper

1 teaspoon chopped garlic

½ teaspoon ground white pepper

½ teaspoon thyme

½ teaspoon oregano

Cayenne pepper to taste

1 lb. smoked sausage

1 lb. bluegill, bass, perch, walleye or crappie fillets

❶ In large skillet, fry bacon over medium-high heat until crispy. Drain bacon on paper towel and set aside. Reserve bacon fat in skillet. Heat bacon fat over medium-high heat until hot; stir in flour, whisking about 5 minutes or until it turns about the color of a brown paper bag. Add chicken broth, vegetables, garlic, white pepper, thyme, oregano and cayenne pepper; cook gently 15 minutes. Add sausage, bacon and fish; simmer 7 minutes or until fish flakes apart easily with a fork. Serve over cooked rice.

8 servings.

FIERY FISH TACOS WITH CRUNCHY CORN SALSA

FIERY FISH TACOS WITH CRUNCHY CORN SALSA

Andrew J. Krotje
Brooksville, Florida

1 cup corn, cooked

½ cup diced red onion

1 cup peeled, chopped jicama

½ cup diced red bell pepper

½ cup finely chopped fresh cilantro

1 lime, peel grated and juiced

2 tablespoons cayenne pepper

1 tablespoon freshly ground black pepper

2 tablespoons salt

6 (4-oz.) tilapia fillets

2 tablespoons olive oil

12 (6-inch) corn tortillas, warmed

2 tablespoons sour cream

❶ Heat grill.

❷ In medium bowl, mix together corn, red onion, jicama, red bell pepper and cilantro. Stir in lime juice and grated peel.

❸ In small bowl, combine cayenne pepper, ground black pepper and salt. Brush each fillet evenly with olive oil and sprinkle with the spice mixture.

❹ Arrange fillets on grill grate; cook over high heat 3 minutes per side or until fish flakes easily with a fork. For each fiery fish taco, top two corn tortillas with fish, sour cream and corn salsa.

6 servings.

SMOKED SALMON CHOWDER

Sue Kelland-Dyer
St. John's, Newfoundland and Labrador, Canada

2 tablespoons butter

2 ribs celery, chopped

1 large onion, chopped

1 green bell pepper, chopped

2 tablespoons all-purpose flour

1½ cups chicken stock

2 cups smoked salmon (preferably Atlantic)

¼ cup sour cream

1 teaspoon fresh dill

¼ teaspoon freshly ground pepper

1 tablespoon chopped fresh parsley

❶ In large saucepan, melt butter over medium heat. Add celery, onion and green bell pepper; sauté 4 to 6 minutes or until vegetables have softened. Add flour and chicken stock, stirring constantly until it comes to a boil. Reduce to a simmer and add smoked salmon, sour cream, dill and pepper. Heat 4 to 5 minutes, stirring constantly. Add parsley before serving.

4 servings.

CREAMY SALMON CHOWDER

Veronica Hill
Emmaus, Pennsylvania

8 cups chicken broth
1 sweet potato, cubed
1 red potato, cubed
2 carrots, sliced
2 ribs celery, sliced
2 leeks, sliced
1 (2-lb.) salmon fillet, diced
1 cup frozen corn
1 can diced tomatoes
2 cups heavy cream
2 bay leaves
2 tablespoons dill weed
2 tablespoons freshly ground pepper
2 tablespoons chopped fresh parsley

❶ In large saucepan, bring chicken broth, potatoes, carrots, celery, leeks and enough water to cover to a boil. Reduce heat and simmer 10 to 15 minutes or until vegetables are nearly soft. Add salmon, corn, tomatoes, cream, bay leaves, dill weed, pepper and parsley; simmer an additional 10 to 15 minutes.

8 servings.

SMOKED SALMON PIZZA

Thomas Lang
Houston, Pennsylvania

1 loaf frozen Italian bread dough
¼ cup olive oil
2 large red onions, sliced in rings
Salt to taste
Freshly ground pepper to taste
2 tablespoons thinly sliced scallions
2 tablespoons chopped fresh parsley
2 tablespoons chopped fresh dill
6 oz. smoked salmon, broken into bite-size pieces
⅓ cup sour cream
6 oz. feta cheese, crumbled
Fresh dill

❶ Thaw bread dough and work into shape of 15-inch round or 12x15-inch rectangular pizza stone. Let dough rest and rise 10 to 15 minutes, reshaping if needed.

❷ Heat oven to 350°F. Bake dough 15 to 20 minutes. Remove from oven just before dough starts to brown. Increase oven temperature to 450°F.

❸ In large skillet, heat olive oil over medium-high heat until hot. Add onions; cook 15 to 20 minutes. Remove skillet from heat. Season onions with salt and pepper.

❹ In medium bowl, combine scallions, parsley and dill; set aside half for garnish. Add remaining half of the scallion mixture to sautéed onions. Spread onion mixture evenly over pizza shell; bake 8 to 10 minutes. Top with salmon pieces, dollops of sour cream and crumbled feta; bake an additional 3 to 5 minutes. Remove pizza from oven; sprinkle with reserved herb mixture. Garnish with fresh dill. Serve immediately with a bottle of semi-dry Riesling. Add yellow or red bell pepper strips or spinach to pizza, if desired.

4 to 6 servings.

HALIBUT GUMBO

Clint Hooper
Camarillo, California

12 cups chicken stock

1 tablespoon chili powder

1 tablespoon file powder

1 tablespoon Tabasco sauce

1 tablespoon salt

½ teaspoon freshly ground pepper

2 cups rice

2 cups chopped onions

2 cups sliced okra

2 lbs. halibut, cut into 1½-inch pieces

❶ In large pot, bring chicken stock to a boil. Add chili powder, file powder, Tabasco, salt, pepper, rice and onions; cook 20 minutes. Add okra and halibut; cook an additional 10 minutes or until fish flakes easily with a fork.

8 to 10 servings.

OAHE WALLEYE CHOWDER

John Brakss
Pierre, South Dakota

¼ lb. butter

3 large onions, chopped

3 quarts water

1 dozen potatoes, diced

2 cans evaporated milk

1 quart fresh milk

3 lbs. walleye fillets, cubed

⅛ teaspoon salt

⅛ teaspoon freshly ground pepper

2 dill sprigs

2 lemon slices

❶ In soup kettle, melt butter over medium heat. Add onions; cook until tender. Add water and diced potatoes; boil about 20 minutes or until potatoes are fork tender. Add walleye cubes and milks; simmer until fish flakes easily with a fork. Add pepper, dill and lemon. Reheat and serve.

6 to 8 servings.

FISH AND POTATO SOUP

Rusty Grohman
La Vernia, Texas

4 medium potatoes, washed and diced

3 to 4 quarts water

4 chicken bouillon cubes

1 teaspoon salt

1 teaspoon cayenne pepper

2 bay leaves

4 tablespoons butter

1 medium onion, diced

1½ to 2 lbs. fish fillets

2 (10-oz.) pkg. frozen corn

❶ In large pot, boil potatoes over high heat. Add bouillon cubes, salt, pepper and bay leaves; boil 15 to 20 minutes.

❷ In large skillet, melt 2 tablespoons of the butter over medium heat. Add onions; sauté until tender. Set aside.

❸ Cut fish fillets into 1-inch cubes and place in skillet with remaining 2 tablespoons butter. Cook until fish is opaque and flakes easily with a fork.

❹ Add frozen corn, sautéed onions and prepared fish to large pot and bring to a boil. Cover pot and simmer 15 to 20 minutes.

4 to 6 servings.

Fish Cooking Techniques

Grilled Swordfish with Rosemary
page 64

North American Fishing Club Members are hooked on fish! Fish complements many flavors, it is quick to prepare and healthy too. Many of our Members practice catch-and-release, but where regulations permit, saving a few "for the pan" is just fine now and then. If you don't keep fish, improved methods of transportation now bring fresh seafood and fish to our local markets from all over the world. So we have a wide variety of choice! We have also learned how to cook fish so that its subtle flavor is enhanced and more intriguing than ever before. Whether you catch fish yourself or become a fish market regular, follow these simple basics for cooking fish.

BBQ Walleye
page 69

Tommy's Baked Trout
page 32

COOKING FISH

Fish is fragile and cooks quickly, so you must be careful and catch it before it becomes dry and over-cooked. As fish cooks, its translucent flesh turns opaque; when it's opaque at the thickest part (test by inserting the tip of a knife), or just slightly translucent at the very center, you know it's done. The fish will be flakey. The Canadian Fisheries Cooking Theory estimates the total cooking time for any fish to be ten minutes for every inch of thickness, measured at the thickest part. This works for whole fish, steaks or fillets, whether grilled, broiled, fried, poached or baked.

Baked & Stuffed

Baking is an ideal cooking technique for fish, as long as you provide some fat or moisture, either in the pan or in a stuffing, to keep the fish from drying out. Whole fish is perfect to bake, but steaks and fillets are fine as well.

To bake a whole fish, remove the scales, guts and fins; keep the head and tail intact unless the fish is very large. Remove the backbone if you are planning to stuff the fish. Stuff the belly cavity with your favorite stuffing—crabmeat or other fish, nuts and crumbs, herbs, greens or vegetables—and secure with butcher twine. Butcher twine is invaluable for tying up whole fish, especially when they're stuffed. Butcher twine is usually available in supermarkets and gourmet stores. Don't substitute sewing thread or yarn—they may contain dyes and solvents not approved for human consumption. Lightly oil the fish and bake it in a preheated 400°F oven in an ovenproof dish, or on a baking sheet lined with aluminum foil, until it is opaque. Aluminum foil is recommended for aiding in the transfer of heat throughout the dish without drying out the fish.

Use butcher twine for tying up fish to be baked; it is approved for use with foods (unlike sewing thread, yarn or household twine).

Baking is done in the oven, thereby surrounding the fish with dry heat. Heat is transferred from the pan to the food and may be further diffused by the use of foil, and layering many ingredients and sauces over the food. In recipes there is usually a range of time but an important basic to remember is that oven temperatures and the temperature of the ingredients vary and pans conduct heat differently, so check the doneness of the fish during the baking process. You can always bake a fish longer, but once it is overcooked you cannot bring it back! Always remember to preheat your oven; many recipes recommend a 350-degree oven for baking the fish. Unless the recipe has lots of layered ingredients, try increasing the oven temperature to 400 degrees and follow the 10-minute-per-inch rule.

When baking fish you should butter or oil the baking dish. If you want the fish to brown slightly use only 2 tablespoons of additional butter or oil in recipe. Keep in mind that the more liquid that you add to the recipe, the more moist your recipe will be. Unless you want your fish to be sauced, keep the liquid to a minimum.

The material of which your pan is made, as well as the size and shape, is important. A shallow, ovenproof baking dish is ideal for baking fish. It is convenient to have ovenproof ware that looks good enough to take to the table. This will help to keep your fish hot and reduce cleanup time later. Many earthenware dishes hold heat well. Individual gratin dishes can be used: simply divide the ingredients in the recipe between the gratin dishes. The baking time will be reduced by 10 minutes.

Broiled, Foiled & Poached

Broiling Fish

Broiling is a particularly successful technique for fattier fish such as salmon, swordfish or shad, since the technique adds very little additional fat. You can broil whole fish, steaks and fillets.

To broil a whole fish, preheat the broiler for at least 15 minutes so that is is very hot. Oil the fish well on both sides and rub it with salt and pepper. Slash the skin in two or three places with a sharp knife, and, if you like, stuff the cavity with herbs, shellfish, lemons or limes. Broil the fish on an oiled rack, 4 to 6 inches from the heat for large fish or 2 to 4 inches from the heat for small fish, until the flesh is opaque. Depending on the thickness of the fish, you may not need to turn it.

Tomato-Orange Fish Fillets
page 50

When broiling fillets or steaks, choose cuts that are at least ³⁄4 inch thick; any thinner than that and they may dry out. Preheat the broiler as for a whole fish. Put the fish in a shallow baking dish and drizzle it with just enough liquid (such as lemon juice, lime juice or white wine) to keep it from drying out. Broil 4 inches from the heat. Thick steaks will need to be turned once; thin steaks or fillets do not need to be turned.

Cooking in Foil

Foil packaging allows fish to steam gently in its own juices. The package can be made from foil or parchment. Cut either foil or parchment into a rectangle or heart shape, and brush the edges with oil. Arrange a thin fillet in the center of one half of the foil or parchment, along with precooked or quick-cooking vegetables, a few tablespoons of liquid, oil or butter, and herbs or spices. Fold the remaining half of the foil or parchment shape over the fish and seal the package by folding in the edges. Cook the packages in a 400-degree oven for 8 to 10 minutes.

Poaching

Poaching is a great way to cook firm-fleshed whole fish or fillets. Lean fish such as halibut or even walleye (whose delicate flesh may dry out over high, dry heat) are perfect for poaching. This is a classic way for preparing fish that is to be served cold.

Poach fish in fish stock made from fish bones, wine, aromatic vegetables and herbs, or a court bouillon made by simmering a combination of water, wine or vinegar, herbs and vegetables for 30 minutes.

To poach a whole fish, place the fish on the rack of a fish poacher. Tie a whole fish loosely to a lightly oiled rack with kitchen string to prevent it from slipping off should the rack tilt when you lift it. Wrap whole fish in cheesecloth for ease of handling. Set the rack in the poacher with the warm court bouillon

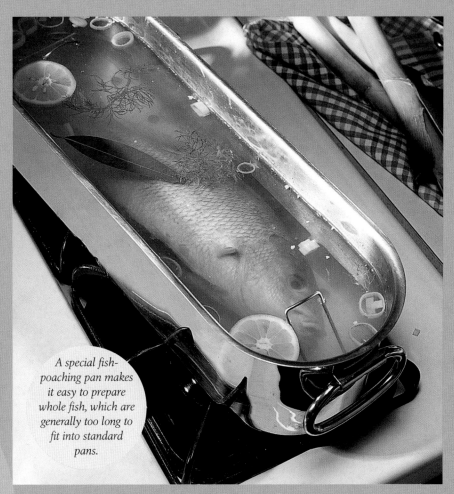

A special fish-poaching pan makes it easy to prepare whole fish, which are generally too long to fit into standard pans.

or stock and bring the liquid to a simmer. Cover the pot and simmer the fish very gently until it is opaque in the center. Begin timing the fish from the moment that the liquid comes to a simmer, and remove the fish immediately from the poaching liquid when it is cooked through. Remove the skin and the fatty brown layer before serving.

Poach fillets in a nonstick skillet. The nonstick skillet is important because fillets are delicate (there are no bones to hold them together) and tend to otherwise stick to the bottom of the pan.

Pan Frying

Pan frying is one of the most popular ways to prepare small fish, fillets or steaks. The outside of the fish becomes deliciously crisp and browned while the inside stays moist and tender. Steaks or fillets from rich fish with more oil can be simply seasoned and fried in about two tablespoons of hot oil. Small, whole fish or fillets of lean fish benefit from the protection of a light crust. Dip the fish in milk or buttermilk, dredge in a starchy coating such as flour, cornmeal, bread crumbs or crushed crackers, and fry in 1/4 inch of oil until the flesh is opaque.

Fry over medium-high heat and use a heavy pan so as not to burn the coating. Use butter or a combination of butter and olive oil. Be careful not to crowd the fish because you want them to brown; cook for about 5 minutes per side. If you have lots of fish fillets cook them in batches. Remove from pan and cover; keep warm in a 325-degree oven until all the fillets are cooked.

Blackened fish is very popular. This method works well with most any fillets, or salmon steaks. Season the fish with a spicy mixture of paprika, onion, garlic, pepper and dried herbs. Then fry in a super-hot cast-iron pan until blackened on both sides.

Make cakes and patties ahead and chill for at least 30 minutes. This allows some of the extra moisture in the cakes to be absorbed by the crumb mixture. Cook the cakes and patties in a mixture of 1 tablespoon of olive oil and 1 tablespoon of butter in a large skillet. Cook the cakes over medium heat until golden on both sides, about 3 minutes per side, adding more oil and butter if necessary. Just as with fillets, if you have lots of cakes and patties to cook, prepare in batches and keep warm in the oven.

A heavy pan is essential for pan frying. Thinner pans buckle and warp, and don't hold the heat well enough for frying.

Deep Fried

Deep-fat frying is best for lean, firm-textured fish. Mildly flavored vegetable, peanut or corn oil, all of which can be heated to a suitable temperature without breaking down, are recommended for frying fish. Use a heavy pot that is deep enough to hold 2 to 3 inches of oil and still be only half full. Cut uniformally-sized pieces of fish, no more than 1 ½ inches thick (any thicker and they will still be raw by the time the coating is cooked). Sprinkle the fish with salt and dip it in any of the following combinations: milk and then flour; flour, then milk, then bread crumbs; or milk, then flour, then beaten egg, then lightly herbed bread crumbs or cracker crumbs.

Heat the oil to between 350 and 375 degrees. Use a thermometer to check the temperature of the oil. (If you are using a deep-fat fryer, this will be regulated.) If the oil is any hotter than this the coating will burn before the fish is cooked; if the oil is cooler the coating will absorb too much oil. Place a single layer of coated fish in the pot. Deep fry the fish in small batches, ensuring they have room enough to spread. Cook the fish, turning them occasionally so that they brown evenly, until the coating is browned and crisp and the fish is cooked through. Timing depends on the size of the fish—a good rule of thumb is about 2 to 3 minutes. Drain and turn out on paper towels. Keep fish pieces warm in the oven and continue frying fish in batches, until all pieces are cooked. Sprinkle with sea salt and serve with lemon quarters.

Mom's Best Crappie Sandwich
page 98

Lake Texoma Spicy Fish
page 13

Grilling

Do not grill or barbecue fish over high heat. Fish should be cooked slowly. Grill fish over subsiding coals and place the fish 5 to 6 inches above the heat. Best results for grilling come when fish is fair sized, at least 1½ pounds in weight.

Turn the fish but once (you may have to use two utensils to keep from breaking the fish in two). With a fish of 1½ to 2 pounds, 7 to 8 minutes per side is recommended. Of course, timing depends on the variable of the heat of your coals. Keep in mind the 10-minutes-per-inch rule. Don't hesitate to cut along the spine into the thickest part of the back to check for doneness. There should be just a hint of translucence in the appearance of the fish. Do not overcook!

Aesthetically, fish should be cleaned, then grilled whole; don't cut off the heads and tails. As for herbs, all of them have an affinity for fish, but be delicate with the use. You can always add more. Salt and pepper can be added after the fish is grilled. Squeeze fresh lemon or lime over the fish before serving.

A grilling basket makes it easy to grill whole fish because it allows you to turn the fish without breaking it up.

You can grill a whole fish fillet without having to turn it. Simply oil the barbecue grate and cover the fish with the lid. For fish steaks, turn the steaks to brown both sides. Follow the 10-minutes-per-inch rule. Experiment with different marinades and seasonings along with charcoals and wood chunks or chips. Grapevine offers a subtle, delicate flavor, but fruit woods such as cherry and apple are the most commonly available wood chips. Their flavor is mild but then produces a sweet, nice wood smoke. If you are marinating fish, keep in mind that fish is delicate and many varieties are soft. Marinate fish for only 20 to 30 minutes. Simply basting the fish with the marinade will infuse flavor.

Another grilling technique utlizes a grilling basket. Because fish are so delicate and can easily break into pieces on the grate, they often benefit from cooking in a grill basket. Choose a basket long enough for your catch. Oil the basket before placing your catch inside, then set the basket on the grill indirectly over medium heat. Use grilling gloves or a hot pad: The handle of a metal grilling basket can get very hot. Also remember to place the basket off the grill grate, thus raising it too far above the fire to be of any use.

Smoked

Smoked fish is great! The smoking process seems to do more for fish than for other meat; smoking not only adds the bouquet and flavor of hickory or whatever other wood you use but, much more importantly, smoking heightens the fish flavor itself. Smoked salmon, for example, has a stronger and fuller salmon taste than fresh salmon. Salmon, trout and catfish also respond well to the smoking process.

For smoking, it is important to read the manual for your own smoker. Smoke-cooking is done between 170 and 250 degrees. The technique to master in smoking, therefore, is keeping the smoker in that temperature range.

For smoking, do not skin or scale fish. Put the dressed fish (fillets or whole) in the brine and sugar solution for 5 to 6 hours. The brine solution is a blend of water, sugar and seasonings. Remove fish from brine solution. Thoroughly rinse out the brine, then roll and pat the fish dry inside and out. Then let it dry in the air for an hour or so. Preheat the smoker about a half hour before you put the fish in.

When the fish is dry; rub with seasonings. Place fish or fillets on the racks, putting the largest fish (or thickest fillets) on the lower racks, and begin smoking. During the smoking process, use wood chunks which you have soaked for at least 1 hour. Shake off excess water before putting the chunks on the coals, and distribute them well to avoid snuffing out any section of the fire. Use long-handled tongs and a mitt for adding wood chunks. As a general rule, start out with no more than 4 wood chunks. When these have burned off, usually after a few hours, add more wood if desired. The more wood chunks you add, the more heavily smoked the food will be.

After about 6 to 7 hours, begin to test for doneness. You'll learn to do this by color eventually, but at first you should do it with a fork: probe a thick section and see if it's done: The fish will flake.

When you remove fish from the smoker, allow it to cool to room temperature, then refrigerate in airtight containers.

Rub seasonings over the fish just before putting it in the smoker. Try mixed herbs and cracked pepper.

Menu Ideas

MENU IDEA

BARBECUE WALLEYE

Entertaining and dining doesn't get any easier than cooking on the grill!

RECIPES

BBQ Walleye (page 69)

Grilled Roasted New Potatoes

Lemon Coleslaw with Caraway Seeds (at right)

Garlic Bread

Watermelon Salad (page 125)

● Roast small new potatoes coated with olive oil, minced garlic, salt, pepper and sprigs of fresh rosemary. Wrap in foil packages and cook over a medium-hot grill for 15 to 20 minutes or until tender.

● Buy your favorite rustic bread, slice, brush with olive oil and grill until toasty brown on both sides. For a garlic flavor, rub the toasted bread with cloves of raw fresh garlic.

● Prepare BBQ Walleye (page 69).

● Serve with Lemon Coleslaw with Caraway Seeds.

● For a refreshing dessert try Watermelon Salad.

LEMON COLESLAW WITH CARAWAY SEEDS

$1/4$ medium red cabbage, shredded, rinsed and dried

$1/4$ medium green cabbage, shredded, rinsed and dried

$1/2$ cup green onion

1 tablespoon caraway seeds

2 teaspoons grated lemon peel

2 tablespoons fresh lemon juice

$1/2$ teaspoon salt

$1/8$ teaspoon cayenne pepper

$1/8$ teaspoon ground white pepper

$1/4$ cup extra-virgin olive oil

❶ In large bowl, combine red cabbage, green cabbage and green onion; toss.

❷ Sprinkle caraway seeds, lemon peel, lemon juice, salt, cayenne pepper and white pepper evenly over the top of the cabbage; toss. Add olive oil, toss again. (Salad can be prepared up to 12 hours ahead. Cover and refrigerate. Bring to room temperature before serving.) (Cabbage will lose volume when dressed.)

4 (1-cup) servings.

WATERMELON SALAD

LIME VINAIGRETTE

2 tablespoons fresh lime juice

½ teaspoon ground cumin

½ teaspoon crushed red pepper

¼ teaspoon salt

2 tablespoons olive oil

WATERMELON SALAD

2 slices (about 1-inch-thick) red, seedless watermelon

2 slices (about 1-inch-thick) yellow, seedless watermelon (or 2 additional slices red, seedless watermelon)

¼ cup fresh cilantro, torn

❶ In small bowl, combine lime juice, cumin, crushed red pepper and salt. Whisk in olive oil.

❷ Using sharp knife, trim rind from watermelon slices. Cut slices into 1-inch-wide strips.

❸ Arrange watermelon strips decoratively on each of 4 salad plates. Drizzle generously with dressing. Sprinkle with cilantro.

4 servings.

BEER BATTERED CRAPPIE

Host a "Fish and Chip Night" at home or at fishing camp!

RECIPES

Beer Battered Crappie (page 10)

Sliced Tomatoes in a Vinaigrette

French Fries

Parsley-Caper Sauce (at right)

Sparkling Mint Limeade (page 127)

- For a quick salad slice vine-ripe tomatoes and dress with your favorite purchased vinaigrette dressing.

- Fries are made quickly by using frozen ones; cook according to directions, drain on paper towels and sprinkle with coarse, kosher salt or make your own salt blend.

- You can make a custom spiced salt for your fries by adding your favorite spice to coarse salt—1 tablespoon chili powder to ⅓ cup coarse salt, for example.

- Make the Parsley-Caper Sauce for dipping your fries in.

- Prepare Beer Battered Crappie (page 10).

- Serve with fresh Sparkling Mint Limeade.

PARSLEY-CAPER SAUCE

2 cups lightly packed fresh Italian parsley leaves

¼ cup drained capers, rinsed

3 garlic cloves, crushed

2 tablespoons vegetable or reduced-sodium chicken broth

1 tablespoon extra-virgin olive oil

1 tablespoon low-fat mayonnaise

1 tablespoon fresh lemon juice

1 teaspoon Dijon mustard

¾ teaspoon anchovy paste

❶ In food processor, combine parsley, capers and garlic; pulse until finely chopped. Add broth, oil, mayonnaise, lemon juice, mustard and anchovy paste; process until mixture forms a creamy sauce, stopping to scrape down sides of bowl several times. (Sauce can be made up ahead. Place sheet of plastic wrap directly on surface to prevent discoloration; refrigerate up to 2 days.)

½ cup.

SPARKLING MINT LIMEADE

1 cup fresh mint sprigs, plus more for garnish
1¼ cups fresh lime juice
⅔ cup sugar
Ice cubes
3 cups (750 ml) chilled sparkling seltzer or soda water

❶ In medium bowl, bruise mint with pestle or wooden spoon to release fragrance. Add lime juice and sugar; stir to dissolve sugar. Cover and refrigerate at least 2 hours or up to 8 hours.

❷ Strain lime juice mixture, pressing on mint sprigs to extract flavor. To serve, place several ice cubes in each of 4 tall glasses. Pour ⅓ cup lime juice mixture into each glass; top off with ¾ cup sparkling water. Garnish each serving with a mint sprig.

4 (1-cup) servings.

BILLY JACK'S CURRIED TROUT

Try this curried fish for an exciting international dinner that every palate will love.

RECIPES

Billy Jack's Curried Trout (page 56)

Jasmine Rice

Sautéed Green Beans with Mustard Seeds

Mint and Ginger Chutney (at right)

Grilled Na'an Bread (page 129) or purchased Pita Bread

Sliced Mango with Lime

- Serve with green beans sautéed in chopped garlic and brown mustard seeds. The mustard seeds will pop when cooked.

- Chutneys are a great condiment for curries; try the Mint and Ginger Chutney recipe. Other condiment ideas include: bowls of raisins, flaked coconut and chopped peanuts.

- Grill your own Na'an Bread outside, on an indoor grill or in a heavy skillet.

- Prepare Billy Jack's Curried Trout. Round out the meal by serving Jasmine Rice.

- For a light dessert slice mangos and top with grated lime peel and a squeeze of lime juice.

MINT AND GINGER CHUTNEY

3 cups lightly packed fresh mint leaves
1 medium jalapeño chile, seeded, coarsely chopped
4 teaspoons coarsely chopped fresh ginger
1 tablespoon sugar
1/2 teaspoon salt
2 garlic cloves, crushed
1/3 cup plain nonfat yogurt
3 tablespoons rice vinegar

❶ In food processor, combine mint, chile, ginger, sugar, salt and 1/2 teaspoon garlic; process until finely chopped. Add yogurt and vinegar; process until mixture forms a creamy sauce, stopping to scrape down sides of bowl several times. (Sauce can be made ahead. Place sheet of plastic wrap directly on surface to prevent discoloration; refrigerate up to 2 days.) Serve at room temperature.

3/4 cup.

GRILLED NA'AN BREAD

1 (¼-oz.) pkg. active dry yeast

1 tablespoon sugar

1¼ cups warm water (105°F to 115°F)

1 egg, lightly beaten

2 tablespoons vegetable oil, plus more for bowl, platter and grill grate

2 tablespoons honey

2 teaspoons salt

4 to 5 cups all-purpose flour, plus additional for dusting work surface

¼ cup (½ stick) unsalted butter, melted, cooled

Olive oil

❶ In large bowl, stir yeast and sugar in warm water until dissolved; let sit 5 minutes to proof, until bubbly. Stir in egg, oil, honey and salt until well combined. Add 3 cups of the flour; mix with wooden spoon until smooth. Add flour in ½-cup increments, mixing with your hands until smooth dough is formed.

❷ Turn out onto lightly floured work surface. Knead 4 minutes by hand, pulling with one hand while pressing into dough with heel of other hand, adding flour in 1-tablespoon increments as necessary to create smooth, non-sticky dough.

❸ Lightly oil large bowl; place dough inside, then turn to coat. Cover; set aside in warm, dry, place about 1½ hours or until doubled in bulk.

❹ Heat grill for direct cooking. Punch dough down; divide into 12 equal balls. Place on oiled platter; cover loosely. Set in warm, dry place about 30 minutes or until puffy.

❺ Brush grill grate with oil. Lightly flour hands. Take 1 dough ball; flatten between palms of your hands, stretching it to 8-inch oval. Place on gas grill directly over medium heat or on charcoal grill 4 to 6 inches directly over medium-hot coals. Cover; grill, turning once, 5 to 6 minutes or until puffed. Brush 1 side with melted butter before serving.

6 servings.

BOURBON GRILLED SALMON

Do your summer cooking outside! The process is fun … and the flavor is exciting.

RECIPES

Bourbon Grilled Salmon (page 94)

Papaya Relish (at right)

Grilled Asparagus

Grilled Tomatoes and Garlic (page 131)

Rice Pilaf

Grilled Summer Fruits served over Ice Cream

- Top this Bourbon Grilled Salmon with a fresh Papaya Relish.

- An easy way to grill asparagus is to thread the spears with water-soaked, 8-inch wooden skewers. Use 2 skewers to thread 4- to 6-spears together going crosswise into the spears, forming a raft of asparagus. Brush with olive oil and season with salt and pepper. Grill 4 to 6 minutes, turning once on a medium-hot grill.

- Continue grilling with a side dish of Grilled Tomatoes and Garlic.

- Serve with a Rice Pilaf and try using some different kinds of rice: wild, brown, black, red or jasmine. For a quicker option, cook one of the many rice mixes on the market.

- Keep on grilling for dessert using sliced fresh pineapple, halved peaches, plums or nectarines. Grill over medium heat 4 to 6 minutes or until caramelized. Serve with your favorite ice cream.

PAPAYA RELISH

    2 garlic cloves, crushed
    2 teaspoons sugar
    1/4 teaspoon salt
    2 tablespoons rice vinegar
    1/2 teaspoon hot pepper sauce
    1 firm papaya, seeded, diced
    1/2 cup diced red onion
    1/2 cup slivered fresh cilantro

❶ Using mortar and pestle or with side of chef's knife, mash garlic, sugar and salt into a paste; transfer to medium bowl. Whisk in vinegar and hot pepper sauce. Add papaya, onion and cilantro; toss gently to mix. Serve within 1 hour.

1 1/2 cups.

GRILLED TOMATOES
AND GARLIC

8 medium tomatoes, cut into halves

4 large garlic cloves

¼ cup olive oil, plus more for grill grate

2 teaspoons salt, preferably sea salt or kosher (coarse) salt

16 basil leaves

❶ Heat grill for direct cooking.

❷ Place tomatoes and garlic in large bowl. Drizzle with olive oil; sprinkle with salt. Toss gently to coat. Thread garlic cloves on water-soaked bamboo skewers; wrap exposed ends of skewer in aluminum foil.

❸ Brush grill grate with oil. Place tomatoes cut-side down and garlic skewer on gas grill directly over high heat or on charcoal grill 4 to 6 inches over high-heat coals.* Cover; grill 3 minutes. Turn tomatoes and garlic with metal spatula; top each tomato half with basil leaf. Grill about 3 minutes or until tomato skins are charred and garlic is browned. Be careful — tomato skins can loosen. Gently transfer tomatoes and garlic to platter.

4 servings.

*Use a grill basket for the tomatoes, but make sure it is thick enough not to crush them when lid is closed. Oil the basket before adding.

MENU IDEA

FIERY FISH TACOS WITH CRUNCHY CORN SALSA

Enjoy this fiesta any season! Tacos are a fun and intriguing way to prepare your catch.

RECIPES

Fiery Fish Tacos (page 109)

Mexican Black Beans (page 133)

Green Rice (at right)

Spiced-Baked Tortilla Chips

Assorted Fruit Slices and Berries

Sangria or Punch

- Prepare Slow Cooker Mexican Beans and Green Rice.

- Make custom Spiced-Baked Tortilla Chips ahead of time: In small bowl, combine 1 teaspoon chili powder, ½ teaspoon cumin and ½ cup olive oil. Cut flour or corn tortillas into wedges or strips; brush with oil mixture and sprinkle with kosher (coarse) salt. Bake at 375°F 5 to 7 minutes or until toasty brown.

- Freeze fruit slices and berries in ice trays to use in your sangria or punch.

- Serve with Fiery Fish Tacos.

GREEN RICE

2 teaspoons olive oil
1 medium onion, chopped
1 (4.5-oz.) can chopped green chiles
2 garlic cloves, minced
1 cup long-grain white rice
1 (14.5-oz.) can reduced-sodium chicken broth
¾ cup chopped fresh cilantro
½ cup chopped trimmed scallions
1 tablespoon fresh lime juice
⅛ teaspoon salt
⅛ teaspoon freshly ground pepper

❶ In medium saucepan, heat oil over medium heat until hot. Add onion; cook about 2 to 3 minutes or until tender, stirring frequently. Add chiles and garlic; cook 1 minute, stirring frequently. Add rice; cook 1 minute, stirring constantly, until well mixed. Add broth; bring to a simmer over medium heat. Reduce heat to low; simmer, covered, about 20 minutes or until rice is tender and liquid has been absorbed. Remove from heat. Add cilantro, scallions, lime juice, salt and pepper; fluff and mix gently with rubber spatula.

4 (1-cup) servings.

MEXICAN BLACK BEANS

2 tablespoons olive oil

1 medium onion, diced

2 (15-oz.) cans black beans, undrained

1/2 cup chopped fresh cilantro

1 tablespoon ground cumin

1/8 teaspoon salt

1/8 teaspoon freshly ground pepper

❶ In large skillet, heat oil over medium heat until hot. Add onion; cook and stir 2 minutes or until soft.

❷ Add beans, cilantro and cumin; mix well. Reduce heat; simmer 15 minutes, stirring occasionally.

8 servings.

MENU IDEA

SALMON BURGERS

Have a build-your-own-burger night with your salmon catch.

RECIPES

Salmon Burgers (page 84)

Spring Time Sauce with Fine Herbs

Sweet Potato Salad (page 135)

Tropical Fruit Salad (at right)

Toasted buns, sliced red onions, sliced tomatoes, pickles, lettuce

Fizzy Ice Tea

● Set up a bar or buffet with all the burger fixings. Let your guests or family members assemble their own Salmon Burgers.

● For a refreshing spread serve the Spring Time Sauce with Fine Herbs.

● The Sweet Potato Salad is a great side. If time is short pick up a potato salad from your local deli.

● For dessert, serve Tropical Fruit salad.

● Put a twist on ice tea: brew a very strong batch, chill and serve over ice with lemon slices, mixing half tea with half lemon-lime soda.

TROPICAL FRUIT SALAD

MANGO POPPY SEED DRESSING

2 ripe mangoes, peeled, pitted

1/2 cup fresh orange juice

1 1/2 teaspoons grated fresh ginger

1 teaspoon soy sauce

Dash salt

1 tablespoon poppy seeds

FRUIT SALAD

2 kiwi fruit, peeled, sliced

1 cup strawberries, hulled, halved

1 small papaya, peeled, seeded and cut into 1/2-inch-thick slices

1/2 cup chopped Maui, Vidalia or other sweet onion

1/2 cup sweetened coconut, toasted

❶ In blender, combine 1 of the mangoes, orange juice, ginger, soy sauce and salt. Cover; blend until smooth. Pour into bowl; stir in poppy seeds.

❷ Cut remaining mango lengthwise into 1/2-inch-thick slices. In large bowl, combine mango slices, kiwi fruit, strawberries, papaya, onion and coconut; toss. Just before serving, add dressing and toss again.

6 (1-cup) servings.

SWEET POTATO SALAD

2 lbs. sweet potatoes, cut into ½-inch-thick slices

1 tablespoon olive oil

1 Maui, Vidalia or other sweet onion, cut into
  1-inch cubes

1 tablespoon olive oil

2 tablespoons water

2 tablespoons extra-virgin olive oil

1 tablespoon fresh lemon juice

1 tablespoon balsamic vinegar

½ teaspoon freshly ground nutmeg

½ teaspoon salt

¼ teaspoon freshly ground pepper

2 tablespoons chopped Italian parsley

❶ Heat oven to 375°F. Evenly arrange sweet potato slices over baking sheet. Drizzle with 1 tablespoon olive oil. Stir potato slices to lightly coat with oil, leaving them in a single layer.

❷ Place onion pieces on another baking sheet. Drizzle with 1 tablespoon olive oil. Stir onions to lightly coat with oil, leaving them in a single layer. Bake potatoes and onions 30 minutes or until potatoes are slightly soft and onions are tender but not brown. Transfer potatoes to large bowl.

❸ In blender, combine onions, water, extra-virgin olive oil, lemon juice, vinegar, nutmeg, salt and pepper. Cover and blend until smooth. Pour over potatoes, toss. Add parsley, toss again.

6 (1-cup) servings.

SMOKED SALMON

Use your own smoked salmon to create this great lunch.

RECIPES

Spinach Salad

Smoked Salmon (page 42)

Crisp Cracker Breads (page 137)

Peach-Blackberry Compote with Basil Syrup (at right)

Fruit Tea

- Combine 4 cups spinach, 1/3 cup minced red onion, 1/3 cup chopped roasted red bell peppers, 1/4 cup chopped olives and 8 ounces flaked Smoked Salmon. Dress with your favorite balsamic dressing and serve with homemade Crisp Cracker Breads.

- For a summer dessert try the Peach-Blackberry Compote.

- For tea with a new twist, add 1 cup fresh fruit that has been lightly mashed to 1 quart freshly brewed tea. Add several sprigs of torn mint and 1/4 cup honey, let it steep until cooled. Serve over ice and garnish with mint.

PEACH-BLACKBERRY COMPOTE WITH BASIL SYRUP

1/4 cup sugar

3 tablespoons dry white wine

3 fresh basil sprigs

2 (2-inch) strips orange peel (thin colored portion only)

3 cups sliced peeled peaches (1 1/2 lbs.)*

1 cup fresh blackberries, rinsed

1 tablespoon fresh lemon juice

Fresh basil sprigs

❶ In small saucepan, simmer sugar and wine over medium heat. Remove from heat; stir in 3 basil sprigs and orange peel. Cover and steep 30 minutes.

❷ Strain syrup into small bowl, pressing on basil and orange peel to release flavor.

❸ In large bowl, combine peaches, blackberries and lemon juice. Add basil-infused syrup; toss gently to coat. Garnish with basil sprigs.

TIP *To peel peaches, dip them into boiling water for a few seconds, and then slip off skin.

4 (1-cup) servings.

CRISP CRACKER BREADS

CRACKERS

2 cups whole wheat flour

1 cup unbleached all-purpose flour

1 teaspoon salt

¼ teaspoon cayenne pepper

2 tablespoons olive oil

1 cup warm water

1 egg white beaten with 1 tablespoon water

TOPPINGS

Kosher (coarse) salt

Sesame seeds

Anise seeds

Cumin seeds

Hulled pumpkin seeds, coarsely chopped

Unsalted sunflower seeds

❶ Place whole wheat flour, all-purpose flour, 1 teaspoon salt and cayenne in food processor. With motor running, add oil and water in steady stream. Process 10 seconds or until ball of dough forms. If dough is too sticky, add a few tablespoons flour. If dough is dry, add a few tablespoons water (you want soft dough).

❷ Process dough about 1 minute longer. Turn dough out onto lightly floured surface. Knead 30 seconds or until smooth and elastic. Transfer to greased bowl; turn dough greased-side up. Cover; let rest 1 hour.

❸ Heat oven to 425°F. Grease 2 large baking sheets. Divide dough into 4 equal pieces. Roll each piece into 10-inch round, about 1/16 inch thick. Transfer to baking sheets. Brush with egg white mixture; sprinkle with desired seed toppings. Bake 12 minutes or until lightly puffed and golden brown.

16 servings.

MENU IDEA

TOMMY'S BAKED TROUT

It won't hurt to save a trout or two where regulations permit. Honor those fish with this wonderful meal.

RECIPES

Tommy's Baked Trout (page 32)

Pepper Pasta Salad with Basil Vinaigrette (at right)

Milanese Focaccia (page 139)

Antipasti Platter

Drunken Fruit

- For a Mediterranean inspired meal, prepare Tommy's Baked Trout stuffed with basil, mint, rosemary and garlic and bake it in wine.

- Serve with Pepper Pasta Salad with Basil Vinaigrette.

- Milanese Focaccia bread can be customized with your favorite herbs: rosemary and thyme. Top it with olives, sun-dried tomatoes or roasted peppers.

- An Antipasti Platter can be quickly assembled from purchased items: mixed olives, canned marinated artichokes, jarred roasted peppers, sliced salami, prosciutto and a variety of cheeses.

- An impressive dessert is easily assembled by scooping 2 to 3 small scoops of purchased fruit sorbet into pretty fluted glasses. Garnish with fresh berries and top off with a splash of sparkling white wine.

PEPPER PASTA SALAD WITH BASIL VINAIGRETTE

BASIL VINAIGRETTE
¼ cup fresh basil, torn
2 tablespoons chopped shallots
1 tablespoon white wine vinegar
½ teaspoon salt
¼ teaspoon freshly ground pepper
⅓ cup extra-virgin olive oil

PASTA SALAD
1 tablespoon kosher (coarse) salt
1 (8-oz.) pkg. penne
2 roasted red bell peppers, coarsely chopped
2 roasted yellow bell peppers, coarsely chopped
2 cups loosely packed baby arugula

❶ In blender, combine basil, shallots, vinegar, ½ teaspoon salt and pepper. Cover; blend until smooth. With blender running, gradually add olive oil.

❷ Meanwhile, fill large pot ⅔ full of water; add kosher salt. Bring to a boil over high heat. Add penne; cook 10 minutes or until al dente. Drain. Rinse thoroughly in cool water; drain. Transfer to large bowl.

❸ Combine vinaigrette and pasta; toss well. Add roasted peppers and arugula; toss again. (Salad can be prepared up to 24 hours ahead. Cover and refrigerate; bring to room temperature before serving.)

6 (1-cup) servings.

MILANESE FOCACCIA

2¼ to 2½ cups unbleached all-purpose flour

1 (¼-oz.) pkg. active dry yeast

2½ teaspoons dried rosemary, crushed

1 teaspoon salt

1¼ cups very warm water (120°F to 130°F)

2 tablespoons olive oil, plus additional for brushing dough

½ cup semolina flour, plus additional for dusting baking sheet

Kosher (coarse) salt

❶ In large bowl, combine 1½ cups of the all-purpose flour, yeast, 1½ teaspoons of the rosemary and salt. Stir in water and 2 tablespoons oil. Beat with electric mixer 30 seconds at low speed; beat at high speed 3 minutes. By hand, stir in ½ cup semolina and enough all-purpose flour to create manageable dough (it will be soft). Turn dough out onto floured surface. Knead in enough remaining all-purpose flour to make medium-soft dough, 3 to 5 minutes or until smooth and elastic. Place in greased bowl; turn dough greased side up. Cover; let rise in warm place 45 to 60 minutes or until doubled in size.

❷ Punch dough down. Spray inside of jumbo resealable plastic bag with nonstick spray. Place dough inside; close bag, allowing room for dough to expand (or keep dough in large bowl). Refrigerate 16 to 24 hours.

❸ Dust large baking sheet with semolina. Remove dough from bag. Place dough on baking sheet. Gently pull and stretch dough into 15x8-inch rectangle. Cover loosely with clean kitchen towel; let rise in warm place 45 minutes or until nearly doubled in size.

❹ Heat oven to 450°F. Using the tips of your fingers, press deep indentations into surface of dough every 1½ to 2 inches. Cover again; let rest 10 minutes. Brush surface of dough lightly with oil; sprinkle with remaining 1 teaspoon rosemary and kosher salt. Bake 16 to 18 minutes or until golden brown. Serve warm, cut into wedges or squares.

12 servings.

RECIPE INDEX

GENERAL INDEX